Dedication

To my wonderful group of students who worked alongside me as I taught, who sometimes asked me to design certain things (like the hedgehog), and who challenged me to try new designs—this book is dedicated to you.

Acknowledgments

I would like to thank the very talented Kris Spray of Stockton, California, for the magnificent job she did longarm machine quilting the top I made. Without the meticulous work she undertook, this quilt would not have gone on to be the award-winning work that it is.

I could not have done the work I did without the support of my husband, Bill, who helped me thrive and defended my stash to his friends, and my family, who understood that quilting wasn't just something I liked to do but rather something I *had* to do. There were many times in the early days of my quilting life that the dining room table was covered in fabric and other quilting materials, to be cleared off only when we actually had to use it or when company was coming over.

I would also like to thank the quilt guilds and quilt stores who are at the root of the industry and who help bring in teachers that inspire and instruct.

Lastly, I would like to thank the entire staff at C&T Publishing for helping me shape the manuscript into a book.

Contents

Preface   6

Introduction   7

A Brief History and Source Inspiration   8

Getting Started   11

Fabric Recommendations   11
- *Choosing Fabrics*   12
- *Choosing Color, Value, and Scale*   15

Tools and Supplies   16
- *Tools*   16
- *Supplies*   18
- *Embellishment Supplies*   19

Techniques   20

Prepared-Edge Appliqué   20
- *Advantages*   20
- *How to Master Prepared-Edge Appliqué*   21
- *How to Glue Appliqué Shapes in Place*   23
- *How to Sew Appliqué Shapes in Place*   24

Making Dimensional Flowers and Pieced Leaves   25
- *Ruched Roses*   26
- *Yo-Yos and Yo-Yo Flowers*   28
- *Pieced Leaves with Textured or Printed Stripes*   30
- *Folded Rosebuds*   31
- *Rickrack Roses*   32
- *Beading and Beaded Berries*   34

Embroidery   35
- *About Embroidery Floss*   35
- *Stitches*   36

Using Ink and Colored Pencils on Fabric   41
- *How to Apply Ink*   42
- *How to Apply Markers*   42
- *How to Apply Pens and Colored Pencils*   42

Gallery of Quilts   43

Seasons of Life   50

Planning the Project: *Seasons of Life*   50
- *Layout Diagram*   51
- *Preparing the Appliqué Block Patterns*   52
- *Cutting the Block Backgrounds*   53

Block Patterns and Instructions   54
- *Spring*   55
- *Summer*   68
- *Fall*   80
- *Winter*   94

Putting It All Together: Making the Quilt Top   106
- *The Center Block: Ruched Rose in a Crown of Flowers*   106
- *Pressing the Blocks and Trimming to Size*   107
- *The Quilt-Top Center*   108
- *Accent Strip and Borders*   108

Resources   110

About the Author   111

Seasons of Life Quilt

Techniques & Patterns for 13 Baltimore Album Quilt Blocks

Sandra L. Mollon

Text copyright © 2021 by Sandra L. Mollon

Photography and artwork copyright © 2021 by C&T Publishing, Inc.

Publisher: Amy Barrett-Daffin

Creative Director: Gailen Runge

Acquisitions Editor: Roxane Cerda

Managing Editor: Liz Aneloski

Editor: Beth Baumgartel

Technical Editor: Debbie Rodgers

Cover/Book Designer: April Mostek

Production Coordinator: Zinnia Heinzmann

Production Editor: Jennifer Warren

Illustrator: Mary E. Flynn

Photo Assistant: Lauren Herberg

Photography by Estefany Gonzalez of C&T Publishing, Inc., unless otherwise noted

Published by C&T Publishing, Inc., P.O. Box 1456, Lafayette, CA 94549

All rights reserved. No part of this work covered by the copyright hereon may be used in any form or reproduced by any means—graphic, electronic, or mechanical, including photocopying, recording, taping, or information storage and retrieval systems—without written permission from the publisher. The copyrights on individual artworks are retained by the artists as noted in *Seasons of Life Quilt*. These designs may be used to make items for personal use only and may not be used for the purpose of personal profit. Items created to benefit nonprofit groups, or that will be publicly displayed, must be conspicuously labeled with the following credit: "Designs copyright © 2021 by Sandra L. Mollon from the book *Seasons of Life Quilt* from C&T Publishing, Inc." Permission for all other purposes must be requested in writing from C&T Publishing, Inc.

Attention Copy Shops: Please note the following exception—publisher and author give permission to photocopy pages 56–59, 61, 64–67, 69–72, 74, 76–79, 82–85, 87, 90–93, 95–98, 100, and 102–105 and pattern pullout pages P1 and P2 for personal use only.

Attention Teachers: C&T Publishing, Inc., encourages the use of our books as texts for teaching. You can find lesson plans for many of our titles at ctpub.com or contact us at ctinfo@ctpub.com or 800-284-1114.

We take great care to ensure that the information included in our products is accurate and presented in good faith, but no warranty is provided, nor are results guaranteed. Having no control over the choices of materials or procedures used, neither the author nor C&T Publishing, Inc., shall have any liability to any person or entity with respect to any loss or damage caused directly or indirectly by the information contained in this book. For your convenience, we post an up-to-date listing of corrections on our website (ctpub.com). If a correction is not already noted, please contact our customer service department at ctinfo@ctpub.com or P.O. Box 1456, Lafayette, CA 94549.

Trademark (™) and registered trademark (®) names are used throughout this book. Rather than use the symbols with every occurrence of a trademark or registered trademark name, we are using the names only in the editorial fashion and to the benefit of the owner, with no intention of infringement.

Library of Congress Cataloging-in-Publication Data

Names: Mollon, Sandra L., 1958- author.

Title: Seasons of life quilt : techniques & patterns for 13 Baltimore album quilt blocks / Sandra L. Mollon.

Description: Lafayette, CA : C&T Publishing, [2021] | Includes bibliographical references.

Identifiers: LCCN 2020046753 | ISBN 9781617459610 (trade paperback) | ISBN 9781617459627 (ebook)

Subjects: LCSH: Appliqué--Patterns. | Patchwork--Patterns. | Album quilts--Maryland--Baltimore.

Classification: LCC TT779 .M65 2021 | DDC 746.44/5041--dc23

LC record available at https://lccn.loc.gov/2020046753

Printed in the USA

10 9 8 7 6 5 4 3 2 1

Seasons of Life Blocks

Spring   55   60   62

Summer   68   73   75

Fall   80   86   88

Winter   94   99   101

Preface

This quilt came to be the same way most things do—with an idea that I would like to try my hand at design.

Detail of *Seasons of Life* by Sandra L. Mollon
Photo courtesy of The National Quilt Museum

Prior to starting this quilt, I worked for more than twenty years making Baltimore Album–style quilts using the *Baltimore Beauties and Beyond* books written by Elly Sienkiewicz. Those books taught me a lot about the types of blocks that comprise an album quilt—like those that form an X shape (great for corners as they draw the eye back into the center of the quilt), those with vases of flowers, those with medallion-style centers, and so many more. I would like to express my gratitude to Elly; I am thankful for her books, which helped to connect contemporary quiltmakers with the women of the mid-1800s. Of course, while making those quilts, my technical skills grew.

Prior to making my first album quilt, I was a beginning quilter and had made only a few quilts. Around that time, the early 1990s, I overheard another member of the quilt guild I had joined call one of my quilts "ugly," suggesting it hang in the back of the show. I was mortified!

Rather than give up and allow a negative comment to deter me from ever making another quilt—something that by this time was bringing me a lot of joy and personal satisfaction—I decided to just create something *better*. I looked through my collection of quilting books and saw pictures of Baltimore Album–style quilts. I had the decided opinion that they were the most beautiful of all the quilts I saw. I spent the next two years diligently working away on (mostly self-taught) hand appliquéing and hand quilting. By the next guild quilt show, I won the Viewer's Choice ribbon and my path as an appliqué enthusiast was set.

Each block in this quilt was individually designed, sometimes wholly from my imagination, other times inspired by other sources, as detailed in A Brief History and Source Inspiration (page 8).

I would also like to share that, as a biology major in college, I simply had no training other than two decades of making blocks and quilts designed by others. Many hours spent tracing shapes onto freezer paper did, in fact, help train both my eye and my hand! With practice and the techniques and designs I share in this book, everyone, with or without quilting experience, can make a beautiful Baltimore Album Quilt.

Introduction

Photo courtesy of The National Quilt Museum

This technique book includes full-size patterns for my quilt, *Seasons of Life*, completed in late 2018 and now a part of the permanent collection of The National Quilt Museum in Paducah, Kentucky. There are fabric recommendations, yardage requirements, and step-by-step directions for prepared-edge appliqué, embroidery (including silk ribbon embroidery), and techniques for using media for realism and shading. If you're already an advanced appliqué quiltmaker, then you may see this book as an additional source of patterns and techniques to add to an existing collection of appliqué designs. Or you may decide to replicate the entire quilt. Whatever your choice, I hope you find this book a source of information and inspiration.

A Brief History and Source Inspiration

One can look back at the mid-nineteenth century Baltimore-style album quilts and see the romance inherent in them. Filled with flowers, wreaths, baskets, cutwork, and pictorial-style blocks, they grew out of the style of *chintz Broderie Perse*, a technique that involves cutting out motifs from printed—and at the time, very expensive—imported fabric and appliquéing them to a less expensive American-produced woven ground cloth. Friendship quilts, signed by the maker (or by one with lovely penmanship on behalf of the maker) in India ink, went hand in hand with autograph books with their sentimental phrases of remembrance.

I eventually noticed the similarity of theorem paintings from the early part of the 1800s to some of the patterns from quilt blocks in the historical Baltimore Album Quilts. A quick glance at theorem paintings from that period would convince anyone familiar with Baltimore Album–style quilts that designers from the height of the album period (1845–1855) did pull elements if not outright designs for their quilt blocks from those paintings. To me, this makes perfect sense. Velvet paintings, done with a series of stencils, or *theorems*, were the fashion for girl's schools between 1810 and 1840. The young women coming into their own homes by mid-century would have likely completed several and been familiar with those designs. (For more information, see *The Art of Theorem Painting*, by Linda Carter Lefko and Barbara Knickerbocker.)

Using that influence myself, I found a theorem painting from the 1830s of a squirrel in an oak tree currently held in the collection of the Oyster Bay Historical Society in Oyster Bay, New York. It was charming, but I felt the squirrel in the painting was a bit out of proportion. I redrew the squirrel using a photo of a real one and couched yarn on the tail, adding a touch of whimsy. Embroidery details are an important part of the style of my work.

Likewise, other influences from later periods inspired my blocks. I love the designs from the early part of the twentieth-century Arts and Crafts Movement.

I used an embroidered cushion-cover design (donated by Annie-May Hegeman to the Smithsonian) as inspiration for my winter block, Arts and Crafts Poinsettia Corner. This design has its origins from William Morris and is currently in the Cooper Hewitt, Smithsonian Design Museum. While not an exact replica, the Arts and Crafts Poinsettia Corner block has the same graceful symmetry of the leaves and flowers. The design gave me the corner shape I needed while staying with my desire to have my quilt reflective of the botanical theme of the winter months.

Cushion Cover, 27 9/16″ × 27 9/16″ (70 × 70cm), mercerized cotton embroidery on cotton, c. 1900

Photo courtesy of Cooper Hewitt, Smithsonian Design Museum

A Brief History and Source Inspiration

The Blackberry Corner block is also from that period. An unknown student from the 1900s did a series of designs based on the blackberry in the style of William Morris, and I adapted one for appliqué and embellished with beaded berries to create a block. The illustrations are in the collection of Sotheby's, London. For more information on Arts and Crafts designs, see Resources (page 110).

Other material inspired me as well. The embroidery of Helen M. Stevens, with its wonderful animals surrounded by graceful arcs of foliage, influenced my designs, including my Among the Foxgloves and Hedgehog in the Garden blocks. And of course the heavy embroidery on my hedgehog is a direct result of the influence of her work.

Detail of hedgehog by Jeanette (Heidi) Gorthy

Sometimes designs came from modern-day magazines with glossy photography. I saw a photo in a home magazine of a collection of antique silver vases with roses in them, and thus Roses in a Silver Vase block came to be. A photo of lush peony flowers, which reminded me so much of my mother's garden, led me to design Peony Vase. But in the end, my biggest influence was the Baltimore Album–style quilts themselves.

Squirrel in Oak, early nineteenth-century theorem painting
Photo courtesy of the Oyster Bay Historical Society

GETTING STARTED

Fabric Recommendations

In this chapter, you will find yardage amounts and a short discussion on suggested fabric types. You will need a variety of fabrics.

MATERIALS

Background: 6–7 yards of 44″- to 45″-wide (or wider) fabric for all appliqué blocks and inner border

Darker value: 3¾ yards for center block, accent strips, and outer border

Appliqué fabrics: 30–40 fat eighths or fat quarters in a variety of colors and textures for appliqués

Backing: 2¾ yards of 104″- to 108″-wide fabric or 8 yards of 44″-wide fabric

Choosing Fabrics

I suggest using either cotton prints, subtle (low-contrast) cotton solids, or silk dupioni for the background fabrics in the blocks and border since they won't compete with the appliqué designs. Be sure to purchase good-quality materials, as not all fabric is created equally and some are not very colorfast or lightfast. I often remind my students that their (and your) investment of time making an heirloom quilt demands that the work stands the test of time. Good-quality fabric then, is a must.

Silk is a wonderful fabric, and its high sheen makes for an eye-catching quilt. I decided to make an all-silk appliqué quilt, but because it does require a bit more care, I recommend you practice sewing with silk prior to using it for the entire quilt. If you love silk as much as I do, I have suggestions on handling it for appliqué (see Silk Fabrics, next page). Many of my students opted to use a cotton background for their blocks and then added a silk border and silk around the center block; they also included both cottons and silk in the appliqués. See Gallery of Quilts (page 43) for examples of their work.

The appliqués *do* lend themselves to silk and other fabrics—much more easily than you might think, and I am hoping with some instruction you will consider adding them to your work. You can, without hesitation, sew silk appliqués on top of a cotton background. See Resources (page 110) for shopping recommendations.

Various silk fabrics prepared for appliqué.

Note: Silk or Faux Silk?

Important note: Be sure your fabric is natural silk, not faux silk, which can handle very differently. If you are not sure of the origins, try a burn test. Outside and with caution, carefully burn a small swatch of the fabric you are considering using. If it produces ashes, it is probably natural silk. If you wind up with a melted lump, it probably is synthetic, and you can then decide if you want to use it or not.

TIP I prewash cotton. It removes the sizing and other glazes from the fabric, preshrinks it, and makes the preparation of the edges easier for appliqué. Since I hand dye most of my own silk and cotton fabrics, they are already washed prior to use. I did not prewash the solid silk dupioni I used in my background.

GETTING STARTED

Silk Fabrics

I credit Hanne Vibeke de Koning-Stapel and her book *Silk Quilts: From the Silk Road to the Quilter's Studio* for giving me permission to try using a variety of silk fabrics. Prior to reading her book, I had the impression that silk was both fragile and difficult to use. Over the past few years I have learned that silk fabrics come in an amazing variety, many hardly fray, they are very durable, they hand dye beautifully, and most are easy to use in appliqué.

Let's get to know some types of silk that I used in my quilt. See Resources (page 110) for information on where to purchase fabrics like these.

CHARMEUSE: This semilustrous fabric has a dull back.

CREPE: This fabric generally features a distinct texture formed by a high yarn twist running in reverse directions in the warp and weft. Thus, the fabric maintains its crepe texture even after washing.

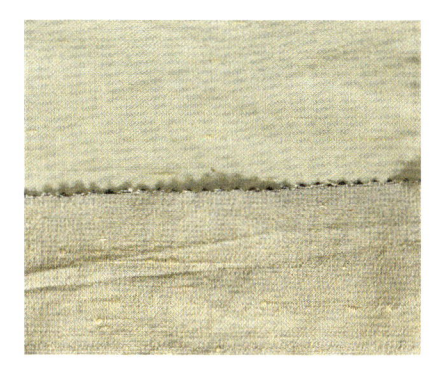

DUPIONI: This fabric is woven from double strands of thread (created by two silkworms nesting together), with areas of nubby texture and a high sheen. If it lacks the characteristic nubby texture but is from China, it may still be called dupioni, as you can see in the two samples pictured.

HABOTAI: This plain, closely woven fabric is both fine and soft with a moderate sheen. Habotai is very lightweight and must be backed with a sheer-weight fusible interfacing to work well in appliqué.

JACQUARD: One of my favorites for texture, jacquard fabric has a pattern woven into the fabric. I have found it in light to medium weights, and the amount of sheen varies with the pattern.

SILK NOIL: This is another one of my favorites because of its coarse texture. Silk noil is woven with yarn from very short silk combings, called *noils*, from the silk cocoons. It is woven slightly thicker than fabrics made from finer silk, and it is decidedly not shiny.

Fabric Recommendations 13

SILK VELVET: This tufted fabric has a short, dense pile and a high sheen. It is usually backed with rayon. The pile is silk, but the reverse side is rayon satin.

SUEDED SILK: This wonderful fabric starts as charmeuse but finishes with a soft, suede-like nap created by sand washing in the finalizing process.

SILK MATELASSÉ: A type of jacquard fabric, silk matelassé has a puffy or cushioned appearance created by a high-relief woven design.

TIPS FOR WORKING WITH SILK FABRICS

Silk can be fine and smooth or coarse and textured; shiny, dull, or suede-like; thin to the point of translucency or fairly thick. Once you are familiar with the types of silk available, you can begin experimenting with them.

- Generally, medium- to heavyweight silk fabrics can be used similarly to cottons without any special handing. I do suggest, however, that when turning the edges for prepared appliqué, you apply spray sizing *very lightly* to the appliqué pieces. I recommend spraying some into a small dish and using an almost a dry brush to apply it to the silk; this keeps the excess sizing from watermarking the fabric.

- If the fabric is very lightweight, you can make it more manageable by fusing an iron-on lightweight or sheer-weight fusible interfacing to the wrong side of the fabric, following the manufacturer's instructions. Once the interfacing is in place, it is suitable for turned-edge appliqués.

- Another option is to apply the interfacing *after* the appliqué shape is turned. Follow How to Master Prepared-Edge Appliqué (page 21) and turn the edges of the silk as instructed. Remove the freezer paper. Carefully cut out a piece of interfacing using the same appliqué template, only cut it about an 1/8″ smaller. Position the interfacing shape, fusible side down, on the wrong side of the appliqué over the turned edges. Press with a hot, dry iron. Try to make sure that none of the interfacing is visible from the front side. This technique produces a silk appliqué that is very easy to hand sew in place, with edges that never turn back out or fray.

- Dupioni, with its wonderful sheen and texture, frays easily. But there are workarounds: When I used it as the background fabric for my appliqué, I serged the edges of the blocks to avoid problems with the final piecing. If you don't have a serger, you can zigzag the edges to minimize fraying.

14   Seasons of Life Quilt

Choosing Color, Value, and Scale

Background fabrics really set the tone, so begin there. Neutral and light-color backgrounds are very common in album quilts. The neutral color and light value allows for a wide variety of color choices in the appliqués and stands out nicely next to darker borders and corners.

While light-value backgrounds allow the appliqué shapes to stand out, another option is black. Very dark backgrounds are dramatic, and colors can really pop. I love the look of clear, bright colors on black.

Center block by Jeanette (Heidi) Gorthy

Among the Foxgloves block by Beth Butera

Sometimes a palette of pastel colors lends an air of softness to a quilt. Personal preferences vary widely. If you are not sure what you like, take some time to research album quilts and find color combinations in quilts that appeal to you.

Once you have chosen the background fabric, you can begin to choose fabrics in a variety colors and values for the flowers, animals, and foliage. I tend to use muted colors and usually stick with more realistic shades—for instance, green for leaves. That being said, there are multiple shades of green, everything from chartreuse to blue-green. Lay out your fabric in color order (use a color wheel) and value order (light to dark). If a particular fabric jumps out or seems out of place, that usually means it is not working well with the others. Set it aside.

Print scale can vary widely. Large floral prints sometimes work if you fussy cut out the motifs to use in appliqués, but this generally results in a lot of wasted fabric. I tend to use more hand-dyed fabrics and soft, almost solid, prints. Hand-dyed fabrics usually have areas that are slightly lighter or darker; with creative cutting, they can be used to add shading and realism to your appliqué shapes.

Tools and Supplies

In addition to general quilting tools, such as rotary cutters and a cutting mat, you'll need a variety of rulers, including long rulers and a square ruler larger than your block size. You'll also need long straight pins, preferably very fine and with glass heads, and a sewing machine to piece your blocks together. Below is a list of the more specialized tools and supplies that will make your quiltmaking and embellishing easier and more professional looking.

Tools

Having the right tools on hand is essential. Here are a few items that make the job easier. I could not do fine detail work without them. See Resources (page 110) for more information on where to find these tools.

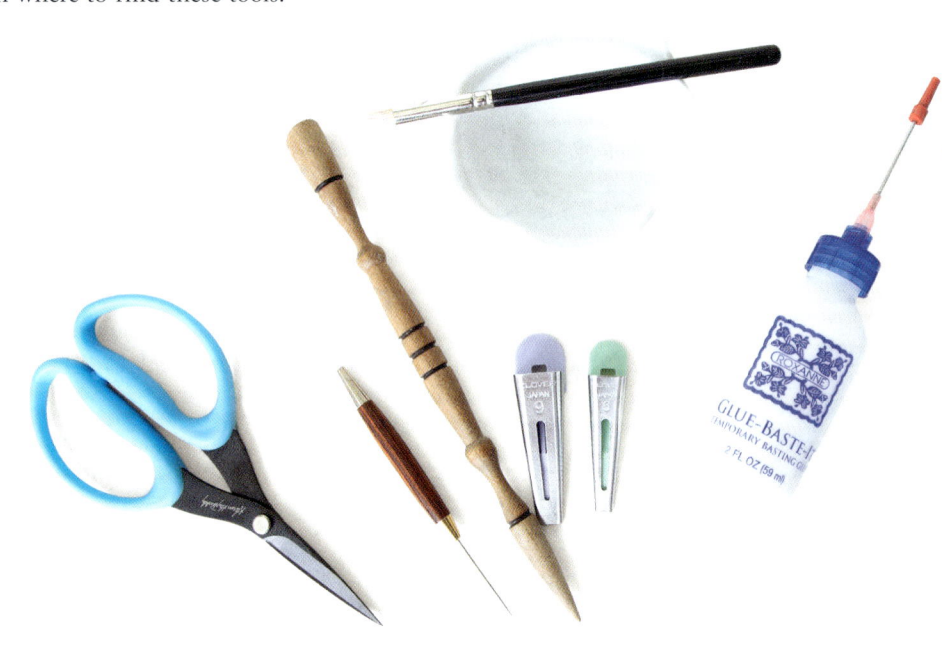

Various tools used for appliqué: fabric scissors, stiletto, appliqué and pressing tool, bowl and stencil brush, bias-tape makers, basting glue, and sizing spray

With a sharp point and a comfortable handle, this stiletto helps me hold and position tiny details, including turning back the dog-ear on a point.

16 Seasons of Life Quilt

GETTING STARTED

Available from P3 Designs, this wooden turning tool helps me to turn deep inside curves and to roll back the edges of the appliqué while pressing with an iron. For tips on using this tool, see Using the Turning Tool (page 23).

Clover Bias Tape Makers in various sizes—including ¼˝ (6mm), ⅜˝ (9mm), ½˝ (12mm), and ¾˝ (18mm)—are always in my toolbox of supplies. See Using Bias-Tape Makers to Make Vines (page 24) and Ruched Roses (page 26) for tips on making vines and roses using bias-tape makers.

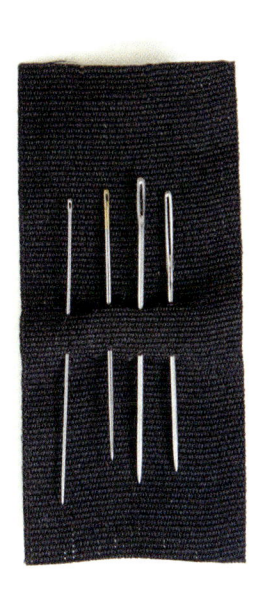

You will need a variety of hand-sewing and embroidery needles. *As shown from left to right:* milliners or straw needle for hand appliqué, sizes 10–11; sharp needle for general hand sewing, sizes 8–10; embroidery needle for hand embroidery using floss or perle cotton, sizes 5–10; and chenille needle for silk ribbon embroidery, sizes 18–24.

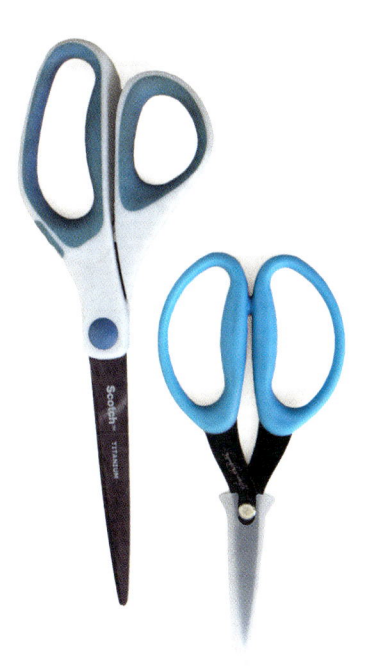

You will certainly need scissors to cut both fabric and paper. My favorite for cutting fabric are micro-serrated scissors. They are lightweight and comfortable, cut smoothly even on fine fabrics, require no sharpening, and are moderately low cost. I use inexpensive 8˝ shears for paper.

Tools and Supplies 17

Supplies

There a few more supplies that will help you. You might find you have most of them already; if not, see Resources (page 110).

SPRAY SIZING is commonly found in your local grocery store, and the brand I use is Magic Sizing (by Faultless). You will also want a small dish or jar to spray it into so you can brush it on the fabric.

A small ¼″ **STENCIL BRUSH** is needed so you can dip into the sizing and apply it to the seam allowance of your fabric when you're using freezer-paper templates for appliqué.

FREEZER PAPER is a must! Also available in most grocery stores, Reynolds Freezer Paper is usually available and works well.

An **IRON** and **IRONING MAT** are also must-haves. I use a small travel iron without steam. I recommend a firm pressing mat such as the Fold-Away Cutting & Pressing Station (by Omnigrid) or a wool pressing mat.

A **PENCIL** is required for tracing the patterns onto the freezer paper. I prefer a mechanical pencil because I don't have to sharpen it, but a regular pencil also works.

A **LIGHTBOX** is essential for tracing when you are making freezer-paper templates because you place your pattern facedown and trace from the wrong side. Using a lightbox is the easiest way to do this.

ROXANNE GLUE-BASTE-IT is my preferred brand of basting glue, and I love it for the fine applicator tip. It holds snugly; however, you can remove the appliqué if necessary by pulling it up. Be sure to use only very tiny dots. It is water soluble, which means that it can be removed with water, and acid free.

#100 SILK THREAD FOR APPLIQUÉ is wonderful. I love silk thread for hand appliqué. It is very fine and smooth, and the thread hides perfectly in the cotton or silk fabric for flawless-looking appliqué. I use YLI and Kinkame silk threads.

#40 OR #50 COTTON OR POLYESTER THREAD is perfect for dimensional flowers. Choose colors that match your fabric.

CRINOLINE is a loosely woven cotton ground cloth onto which dimensional flowers are sewn. You will need only a small 2″–3″ square for each flower. Once the bulky flowers are sewn to the crinoline, they can be positioned onto your background and easily stitched in place.

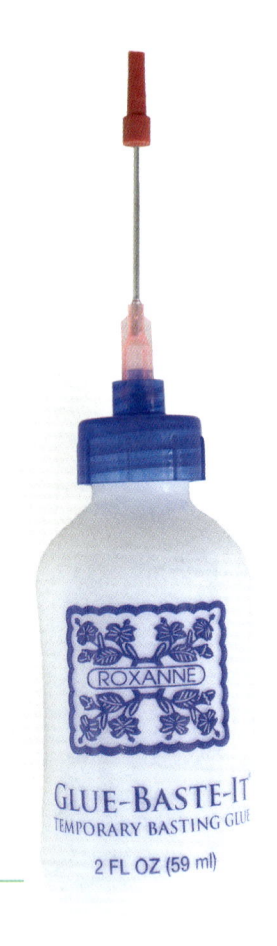

GETTING STARTED

Embellishment Supplies

Embellishing your quilt is half the fun! This particular quilt is like a controlled crazy quilt. The details enrich the visual experience and add special touches. Most embellishments are simple to use once you learn the techniques. This is the list of items you may want to have on hand to make the *Seasons of Life* quilt.

ULTRASUEDE is a synthetic ultra-microfiber sold as a substitute for suede leather, the only man-made fiber I really love. Because it is highly durable and colorfast, and does not fray, it is perfect for small pieces which would otherwise be difficult to turn. You can cut it out in the exact size you need, and it will appliqué in place beautifully by hand using the same thread as for cotton or silk. Because of the expense, I purchase it in small (9″ × 12″) pieces. I used beige, red, gray, teal blue, various greens, black, gold, tan, and brown in this project.

WOOL FELT was used as a base to sew my beaded berries. I used small circles of red or off-white wool felt. Once the quilting was complete, I carefully sewed them to the quilt's top layer, trying not to go through to the back.

BEADS can be sewn on using milliners needles, but a sturdy **BEADING THREAD** is essential. I use Nymo beading thread in size D for most of the bead work, it comes in a variety of colors; use a color matching the bead color. The beads I use vary from size 8 to 11.

SILK RIBBON was mostly used in sizes from 4mm to 7mm wide for this project. Solid colors or hand-dyed ribbon are available. I find that the ribbons manufactured in Japan tend to be higher quality than ribbons manufactured in China, but both are suitable. In my quilt, I used various greens, hand-dyed pink to green, reds, and yellow to yellow-orange. See Resources (page 110).

EMBROIDERY FLOSS can be silk or cotton, a solid color, variegated, or hand dyed.

TIP I have experienced hand-dyed cotton floss bleeding when it gets wet. You can eliminate this problem by testing the floss: Wet a piece of the floss you plan to use and lay it on a light-color fabric scrap to see if bleeding is an issue. While you can wash floss, frankly it's a hassle. I just don't use any floss that bleeds.

ELLY'S EMBELLISHMENT THREAD (BY YLI THREADS) is a lovely #30 variegated silk thread that can be used single stranded to hand embroider. It has a high sheen.

COLOR INFUSIONS MEMORY THREAD (BY DMC), or any type of gimp cording that has a fine wire inside to allow for shaping, is helpful for some block elements. I used the thread in medium gray for the body of my dragonfly.

PERLE COTTON comes in a variety of sizes and colors. I recommend sizes 8–10 in the colors of your choice. It can be used instead of floss for hand embroidery and has the advantage of being a single strand that doesn't need to be divided.

ALL-PURPOSE INK AND FABRICO MARKERS (BOTH BY TSUKINEKO) can add subtle shading without changing the hand of the fabric, and the ink is colorfast when heat set. I used the inks in #80 White, #66 Thyme, #74 Champagne Mist, #52 Sand, #81 Cool Gray, #55 Truffle, and #60 Celadon. The markers have the same-color ink, numbers that coordinate (with a number starting with 1 in front), and the same color names. For example, #52 Sand in the bottle is number #152 in the marker. I recommend having the above colored markers on hand. Note that white and metallic colors (Champagne Mist) do not have coordinating markers available. See Using Ink and Colored Pencils on Fabric (page 41).

COLORED PENCILS are easy to use on fabric, and they softly enhance color or shading. I recommend a good-quality set like Prismacolor or Faber-Castell.

EYELASH YARN adds dimension, like here, where I couched it in place on the squirrel's tail. This small detail adds a lot of texture and fun to the block.

Tools and Supplies 19

Prepared-Edge Appliqué

There are several advantages to prepared-edge appliqué over needle-turn appliqué. I used prepared-edge appliqué and freezer-paper templates to make the appliqués in this book. The freezer-paper templates are fairly durable and can be reused several times to make appliqués of the same shape.

Advantages

- First, I find it very fast to hand appliqué. All the edges are turned under and lightly glued to the background before you begin to sew, so you don't have to struggle to match a line, fiddle with the seam allowance, or mark your background.

- More importantly, though, you can prepare all the pieces for a particular block and "glue assemble" them into units. This makes appliquéd motifs like roses easier to place accurately on the background because all of the loose petals are first glued to each other. This also shows you what the final block will look like prior to hand sewing. Nobody really likes to rip out finished work!

- Once the appliqués are positioned on the background fabric, you can evaluate the fabric choices and make any changes quickly and easily.

- Lastly, and perhaps most importantly, the appliqué is very precise. This method produces very smooth curves, sharp points, and deep inside curves without fraying—all hallmarks of fine appliqué.

TECHNIQUES

How to Master Prepared-Edge Appliqué

If you are new to making appliqué, I recommend that you first do a practice shape like this heart, with its outside curves, inside and outside points, and straight edge as demonstrated in the following steps. Draw a heart to use as a pattern.

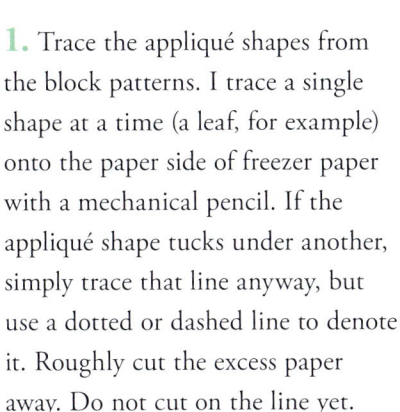

1. Trace the appliqué shapes from the block patterns. I trace a single shape at a time (a leaf, for example) onto the paper side of freezer paper with a mechanical pencil. If the appliqué shape tucks under another, simply trace that line anyway, but use a dotted or dashed line to denote it. Roughly cut the excess paper away. Do not cut on the line yet.

IF YOU HAVE A LIGHTBOX, trace from the reverse or wrong side of the pattern by placing the master pattern facedown on a lightbox.

IF YOU CAN PRINT A MIRROR IMAGE OF THE PATTERN, then you trace from the right side. You may not need a lightbox.

2. Place the first piece of freezer paper on top of another blank piece of freezer paper of a similar size, with both shiny sides down. Press with a hot iron. The purpose of this step is to produce a thick paper template that will help it stand up to use or possibly multiple uses. Be sure to keep both shiny sides of the paper facing down. You can press this directly on top of your ironing board or mat without worry. It will peel right back up without damaging the surface.

3. Cut out the shape on the drawn line with paper scissors. Cut smoothly, holding your scissors up in front of you and turning the paper. When you come to a dashed or dotted line (which designates a piece that tucks under another), cut slightly outside the line. I find that cutting directly on a dashed line obliterates it, and I want to be able to see it.

Prepared-Edge Appliqué 21

4. Press the freezer paper to the wrong side of your chosen fabric. The plastic-coated side of the freezer-paper template sticks wonderfully but not permanently to your fabric, silk, or cotton when pressed on with a hot iron. This helps hold it snugly while cutting. Trim away the excess fabric, leaving a scant seam allowance of ¼″ to just over ⅛″ for very small shapes.

If after cutting the seam allowance you are left with a longish triangle at the outside point, clip it back to ¼″ but do not cut if off entirely (note the point of the heart sample). You want fabric there to turn back without leaving a frayed tip.

TIP Do measure and mark your seam allowance if you are a beginner. Many of my beginning students tended to cut an oversized seam allowance because they were fearful of cutting too close. But in my experience, having the correct seam allowance matters. Too much fabric is much more difficult to deal with and the resulting work less pleasing.

5. Apply sizing to the seam allowance. I prefer spray sizing over spray starch of any type. Aim the spray into a small dish and collect a tablespoon or so to use when you are ready to turn the edges of your appliqué. Dip your small (¼″) stencil brush into the liquid sizing and lightly paint it on the exposed seam allowances.

TIP I discovered that if spray sizing sits around for a few hours, it evaporates slightly, leaving a slightly thicker product that is much stickier and easier to use on silk.

6. Test how well the fabric turns back over the freezer-paper template with your fingers. If it turns back easily, do not clip into the seam allowance. If it doesn't, make as many clips as needed to turn it back—usually 1–3 clips. Only clip inside curves; *trim outside points to ¼″*. Remember: *Do not clip outside (convex) curves.* This can lead to minor fray at the edge in those spots.

7. Press the seam allowances back over the freezer paper. With the fabric side down on your pressing mat, freezer-paper template up, coax the seam allowances of the fabric back snugly to the paper. Using your fingers or the stiletto, and with an iron in your other hand, press with your hot, dry iron. If it doesn't stick to the freezer-paper template within a few seconds, your iron probably isn't hot enough. Make sure all edges are snug to the paper, all the way to the point. Outside curves should be smooth, the seam allowance forming what appears to be gathers over the freezer paper, with no pleats that form points. If you get some pleats that form little points in the curve, simply remoisten that spot, tug it out with your stiletto and press it back into place. See Tips for Working with Silk Fabrics (page 14).

22 Seasons of Life Quilt

TECHNIQUES

8. Sharp points are a hallmark of good appliqué. Once most of the turning has been done on any shape, I finish off the points. Apply a *small* dot of glue on the tip of the seam allowance. Grab it with your stiletto and fold it back to form your finished point. Hold for a second for the glue to adhere. Do not use a lot of glue! It would be messy and hard to hand sew through. Voilà! You have a sharp point. Remove the freezer paper by gently pulling it away.

TIP ✄ Using the Turning Tool

If your appliqué shape has deep inside curves, the wooden tool helps you turn those smoothly. While the freezer paper is in place, clip the seam allowance nearly to the paper and apply sizing lightly. Starting from the front of the appliqué, place the rounded tip into the curve and use it to roll back the seam allowance. Press with your iron right on top of the tool to help set. Then remove the tool and finish pressing from the paper side.

How to Glue Appliqué Shapes in Place

1. Lightly crease your background fabric to find the center of the block. Fold the square in half, crease the center lightly with your fingers, and then fold in half in the other direction and crease again. This will lightly mark the center point of your fabric.

2. Place your master pattern on a lightbox and lay your background fabric on top, right side up. Match the center of your fabric square to the center of the pattern. Pin the background fabric to the paper while you are gluing the appliqués in place.

3. Carefully position the appliqué shapes where they go. You should be able to see your pattern through the fabric when it is on the lightbox—if not, darken the room lights. Apply tiny dots of glue on the seam allowance by lifting the folded edges a little at a time. Then press the appliqué down with your fingertips onto the background fabric.

Note

For complex shapes with multiple pieces, I approach the gluing a bit differently. I place the individual pieces on the right side of the master pattern and glue them to the adjacent piece until I have the completed complex shape, taking care to overlap the raw edges of the adjacent piece, like the petals of the layered rose. Take care that you only glue the pieces to each other and not to the paper. Then you can lift the fully assembled shape and, following the directions above, glue it lightly to the background fabric.

Prepared-Edge Appliqué

USING BIAS-TAPE MAKERS TO MAKE VINES

Bias-tape makers are very helpful for making vines and ruched roses.

Fabric strips for vines that need to curve are cut on the bias (45° angle) of the fabric. The give, or stretch, of the bias helps your vines curve easily yet lie flat on the background.

Cut your fabric strips exactly *twice* the size as the bias-tape maker you are using. For example, cut your strip ½˝ wide for use in the ¼˝ bias-tape maker. Use a rotary cutter, ruler, and mat to cut even-width strips.

Insert the strips in the bias-tape maker and then press the folds. Be sure to keep your iron close to the tip of the bias-tape maker.

How to Sew Appliqué Shapes in Place

Of course, appliqué is not permanent until you stitch it into place. I sew by hand using the invisible tack stitch.

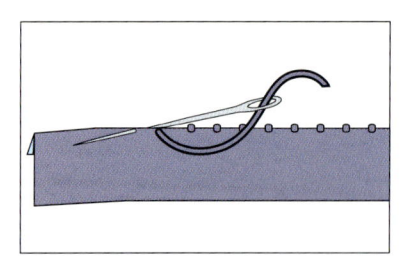

Use a fine milliners or straw needle and a fine thread (like the #100 silk thread) in a color that matches the appliqué (not the background) or in a neutral color like gray or beige, which hides nicely. Thread length should not be much longer than 18˝. Thread the needle and tie a quilter's knot on the end. To tie the knot, hold the needle in one hand, and with your other hand, wrap the end of the thread around the needle a few times. Hold the wraps and pull the needle through, sliding the wraps down the thread to the end, where they should form a small round knot.

I am right-handed, so reverse these instructions if you are left-handed. I sew with my left hand holding the fabric and my thumb on top of the work. My right hand holds the needle. Starting from the underside of the block, bring the needle up, catching just a few threads on the fold of the appliqué. Position the needle in the background fabric exactly *beside* the place you came up; then push forward a bit until you come up ⅛˝ or less in the fold of the appliqué. The needle pushes, but your other hand has a very important role here, too. It supports the work, and as you push the needle forward, your thumb pushes down on your fabric slightly to form the stitch length. Harmony in sewing, speed, and even stitch length are determined by this flow between your hands. It comes naturally with practice.

TECHNIQUES

Making Dimensional Flowers and Pieced Leaves

Dimensional flowers and leaves take extra time to make but add so much texture to the block. Viewers often marvel at the result and wonder how it is done. The following instructions show you how to make some of the flowers and leaves I use most often.

When you have completed the dimensional flowers or pieced leaves, simply pin them in place and stitch them to the background fabric, catching just the edges. Use the same appliqué stitch for the dimensional flowers as any other appliqué motif, but make sure that the background fabric continues to lie flat beneath the dimensional flower. As your needle catches the edge of the bottom of the dimensional flower or rosebud, take care that you are not drawing up extra background fabric beneath. Check your background fabric often from the reverse side to see that you have not inadvertently sewn in a fold or crease.

Detail of center block by Sandra L. Mollon

Photo courtesy of The National Quilt Museum

Ruched Roses

This lovely dimensional flower appears in the center block. Making it is simpler than it looks. Mine was made from a medium-weight silk jacquard fabric, but cotton fabric works just as well. The rose featured in the photos is made with an ombré cotton batik.

You'll need the following: a fabric strip at least 1¼″ wide, a ¾″ bias-tape maker, paper and a pen, a fabric marker or chalk, a safety pin, quilting pins, a scrap of crinoline the same approximate size as the finished flower, thread, and a hand-sewing needle.

1. Cut a 1¼″-wide strip of fabric from selvage to selvage (not cut on the bias), about 44″ long. Lightly spray it with sizing until it is slightly damp, and run it right side up though the ¾″ bias-tape maker, pressing as you go. Be sure to keep your iron right next to the tip of the bias-tape maker so that the folds are firmly pressed. The strip will now have a right side without raw edges and a wrong side with the raw edges folded in towards the center of the strip.

2. On the right side, starting about ½″ in from one end, make small marks in 1″ increments with a white, silver, or regular pencil along one edge. On the other edge, starting in about 1″, also mark in 1″ increments, but these should be staggered ½″ from the other side.

3. Sew a running stitch using a single strand of thread, about 4 stitches per inch. Use cotton or polyester thread in a sharps size 10 or embroidery needle size 10. Sew from tick mark to tick mark, forming a zigzag pattern as you sew.

4. After you have sewn about 4″–5″ along the strip, pull the thread gently to gather. Keep up this pattern of sewing for a few inches and then pulling to gather until the entire length is gathered. Knot off.

26   Seasons of Life Quilt

TECHNIQUES

5. Draw a circle on a piece of paper the same approximate size as the flower you plan to make. Place one end of the gathered strip in the center and pin it to the paper, bringing the pin in from the back of the paper.

TIP How firmly you gather depends on individual taste. Looser folds form softer curves. Folds pulled tightly are more oval shape, and the overall length of the gathered strip is proportionately shorter and the resulting flower smaller.

6. Wind the strip around this center, carefully underlapping the previous rows. When you reach the end, simply tuck it underneath. Now place one hand on top of the flower, pressing down to hold the rows together, and insert long pins from the outside edge towards the center all around the flower. I use about 10–15 pins for this.

7. Remove the pin on the back of the paper to release the flower. It should hold its shape nicely because of the pins on top, and you can gently coax it into a nice circular shape. Cut out a circle of crinoline just slightly smaller than your flower. Pin it to the back.

8. Appliqué the flower to the crinoline by taking vertical stitches, going up to catch a petal and then back into the crinoline, until the flower is firmly attached. When this is complete, place the flower onto your background fabric and appliqué the final edge in place. Be sure to complete any leaves that tuck under the flower first.

Making Dimensional Flowers and Pieced Leaves

Yo-Yos and Yo-Yo Flowers

Yo-yos have been around for a long time. You do not need any special tools to make them, although a circle template helps.

Making a Yo-Yo

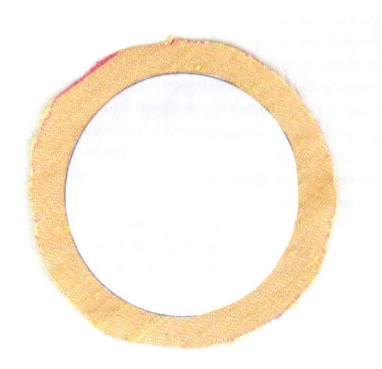

1. Determine how large you want your yo-yo to be and draw a circle on a piece of freezer paper exactly *twice* that size. For example, a 1″-diameter yo-yo requires a freezer-paper template 2″ in diameter. Once you have that, press it to your fabric with a warm iron and cut it out, adding a ¼″ seam allowance in your fabric.

2. Press the seam allowance onto the freezer paper in the same way as for prepared-edge appliqué. Remove the freezer-paper template.

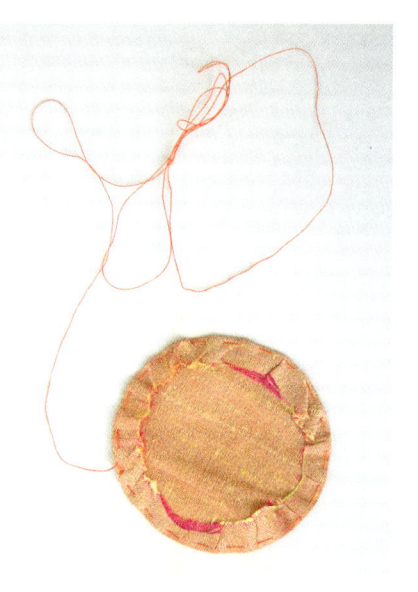

3. Tie a knot at the end of a single strand of thread. Stitch a running stitch (stitches should be about 5–6 per inch) using a single sturdy thread around the edge of the circle, close to the fold.

4. Pull to gather the thread and form the yo-yo. Bring the thread to the back and knot off. The yo-yo is now ready to appliqué in place on your block.

Making a Yo-Yo Flower

After gathering the yo-yo, simply wrap the thread back over the edge and bring the needle back through the center hole from the front. Repeat 4 more times for a total of 5 wraps, making them as evenly spaced as possible and pulling snugly to form the petals, and knot off.

28 ❀ Seasons of Life Quilt

TECHNIQUES

Making a Fringed Flower Center

In the Magnolia Vase block, I added a strip of frayed yellow cotton fabric behind a yo-yo to make a fringed flower center.

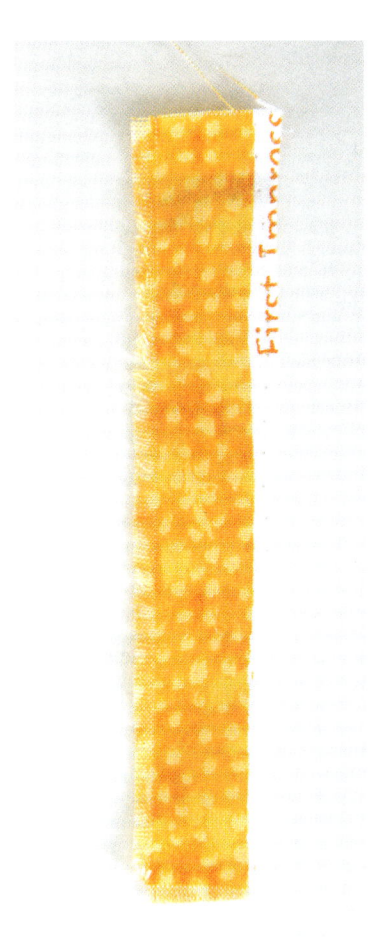

1. Cut a strip of fabric from the selvage edge of a loosely woven cotton fabric. The strip should be 4″–5″ long with about a ½″ of fabric extending beyond the selvage edge.

2. With the point of your stiletto, pull out the threads that run parallel to the selvage, leaving the cross woven threads. Sew a line of running stitches through the selvage using a single thread.

3. Pull the thread to gather the strip and sew the ends together into a circle.

4. Place the fringed circle behind a yo-yo and stitch the yo-yo into place; the stitching holds both the frayed circle and yo-yo in place. You can trim the frayed threads evenly if desired.

Detail of Magnolia Vase block
by Sandra L. Mollon
Photo courtesy of The National Quilt Museum

Making Dimensional Flowers and Pieced Leaves

Pieced Leaves with Textured or Printed Stripes

Using a silk crepe (shown above), ribbed silk (also shown above), or a woven or printed cotton fabric with narrow stripes, you can make leaves that mimic nature, with lines that form a chevron along a center vein.

1. Determine the width of the leaf you wish to make so you cut your strips wide enough. For a leaf 2″ wide at its widest point, divide this width in half and add ½″ for a seam allowance on each side. For this example, cut 2 strips at least 1½″ wide.

2. To cut the strips with angled stripes, place your fabric on a cutting mat. With your ruler at a 45° angle to the edge, cut off first a triangle and then subsequent strips. On an opposite corner, do the same, but cut your 45° angle mirror-image to the first cut. You will have strips with the lines running at opposite angles.

3. With right sides together, align the strips so that the lines in the fabric form a chevron. Machine stitch with ¼″ seam allowance.

4. Press the seam allowances open. Press the desired freezer-paper leaf template on the wrong side, placing it so that the seam is in the center. Treat it the same way you would for prepared-edge appliqué to finish the edges.

30 ❦ Seasons of Life Quilt

TECHNIQUES

Folded Rosebuds

Folded rosebuds add interest with texture and dimension, and they are easy to make.

1. Draw a 3″- to 4″-diameter circle on fabric using a pencil and a circle template. Cut on the drawn line.

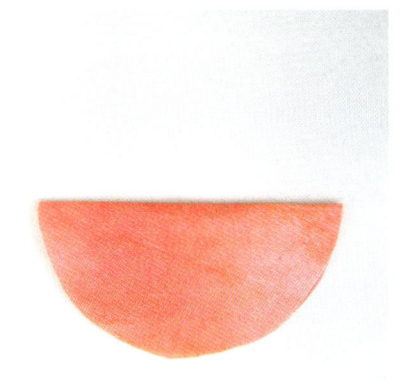

2. Fold in half to form a semicircle.

3. Fold the sides in from the left and then from the right to form the top of the bud.

4. Using a single strand of sturdy thread, like a #40 cotton, hand sew a running stitch along the bottom edge.

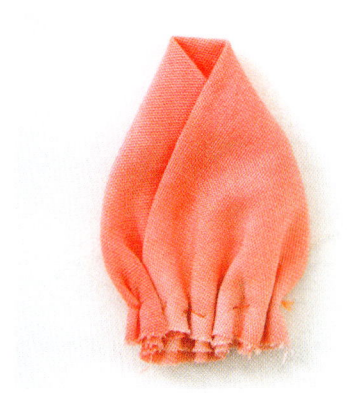

5. Pull the thread to gather, doubling back towards the center, and knot off. The unfinished bottom edge will be covered by a calyx, often cut from Ultrasuede.

TIP When using a finely woven silk fabric, cut a piece of sheer-weight fusible interfacing the same shape but slightly smaller all around than the finished leaf. Fuse it to the wrong side of the leaf. The interfacing holds the raw edges in place and helps the leaf maintain its shape, even for fussy fabrics like the silk crepe shown here.

Making Dimensional Flowers and Pieced Leaves 31

Rickrack Roses

Ruched rose with rickrack center

Rickrack trim has been used for decades as a trim for clothing. I have used various widths of rickrack woven into basket-trim details in quilt blocks and for the center in ruched roses, as seen here, for many years. It always adds interest and is fun to work with.

1. Start with a length of rickrack about 1½ yards long. The length is somewhat variable. I have done this with leftover scraps of short lengths and to make the center of a ruched rose. The width of rickrack available on the market also varies. For small flowers, I love rayon rickrack that is only ⅛″ wide. Try making a flower out of whatever size you have on hand. Fold the length in half, and weave by wrapping one side around the other, locking both together, until the entire length is braided.

2. Roll the rickrack into a small ball starting at the folded end. This forms the flower center.

TECHNIQUES

3. Look at both sides of the ball and decide which is the right side. Use a single strand of a sturdy cotton or polyester thread and a sharp needle to sew a few whipstitches on the wrong side of the ball, holding the center in place. With the remaining thread still in place on your needle, sew a row of running stitches, going in and out of each point on one side of the remaining strip.

4. Pull the thread to lightly gather. Wrap the gathered rickrack around the ball, forming the remaining petals, and pin in place, tucking the raw ends to the back. Whipstitch together.

5. Your rose is now ready to appliqué in place on your work.

Making Dimensional Flowers and Pieced Leaves

Beading and Beaded Berries

Detail of the Blackberry Corner block by Sandra L. Mollon
Photo courtesy of The National Quilt Museum

Beading is a fun way to add interest and sparkle to a block. Beads also add dimension and realism. It's fairly easy to add them, and it goes quicker than you may think. Be sure to use Nymo or similar beading thread and a #11 milliners or beading needle.

Making Beaded Berries

1. Cut a small oval of wool felt in a color similar to the finished berry. Cover it with as many beads as desired, using the bead stitch and beading thread. For a berry, it is best to cover the felt completely, nearly to the edges.

2. If you cover the entire layer of felt and want to add a few beads in the center to rest on top of the first layer of beads, be sure to pass the thread through the top layer of beads as well as random beads on the bottom layer. Add a few backstitches behind the work in the felt as you bead; this prevents all the beads from coming loose in case of a broken thread.

TIP Set aside all beaded berries until your quilt top is completely quilted. Appliqué them in place on the quilt, but carefully avoid stitching all the way through to the back of the quilt by catching your stitches on the felt only and the top layer of the fabric background.

Beading Stitches

You can sew beads to the fabric one at a time or in rows.

SEWING A SINGLE BEAD

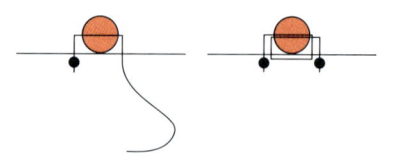

Secure your threads with several backstitches or a single knot on the wrong side, and then bring your thread up from behind your work. Pass it through the bead and then back down into the background fabric or felt. You can then continue adding single beads as desired or knot off.

SEWING ROWS OF BEADS

Start by securing your thread on the back as directed above; then pass your thread through a few beads. When adding short rows, come back up from the back again and pass though some of the beads to reinforce your line.

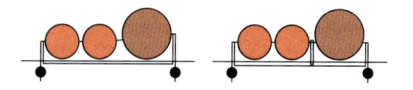

Seasons of Life Quilt

TECHNIQUES

Embroidery

Photo courtesy of The National Quilt Museum

Embroidery adds so many important details to this quilt, and it is a pleasure to work. I often find myself embroidering while relaxing with my family or when I am otherwise unoccupied. I hand embroidered the monogram in the center of the quilt using a series of steps known as French Laid embroidery. I do not offer monograms here, as many books have wonderful examples for you to see. See Resources (page 110) for books with full-size monograms to trace.

Note: Color Choices for Embroidery Floss and Silk Ribbon

In my experience teaching hand appliqué with embroidered details, I find that color choices for the floss and ribbon are best chosen by auditioning the color in coordination with the block. Lay the thread on top of the fabric you chose to use for your appliqué. Does it coordinate well? Are the value differences enough for it to show? I don't often give specific color recommendations in this book because much depends on your individual choice of fabrics.

About Embroidery Floss

Embroidery floss usually comes in skeins with six strands, although you can purchase two-stranded floss. Always separate the strands, pulling one at a time from your cut length. If you are using two strands to embroider (which I often do), then lay them side by side in the direction that you pulled them from the skein.

Floss Direction

Floss and threads are manufactured with a twist and sew more smoothly in one direction along its length than the opposite way. To find the twist direction, take a single strand of floss and drag it gently between two fingers; then repeat going in the other direction along the length. One direction should feel smoother than the other. Use that direction while sewing.

Embroidery 35

Stitches

Backstitch

Backstitch is used to make a line or outline an appliqué shape.

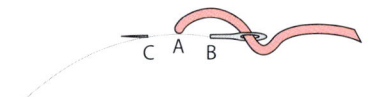

1. Draw a fine line in pencil on your block to help guide your stitches. Bring your thread up at A and down about ⅛″ away; insert at B. In the same motion, come up at C, just slightly ahead of A.

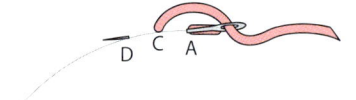

2. Reinsert your needle at A coming up at D.

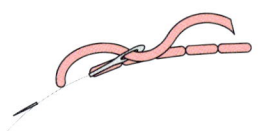

3. Continue until your design line is complete.

TIP 🌀 I like to begin and end any type of hand embroidery with a few backstitches. Use the stitches to lock threads to the wrong side of your block instead of using a knot. Catch a small amount of fabric with the needle on the wrong side your fabric and make 3–4 stacked backstitches. The stitching should now hold without coming undone.

Bullion Knot

Detail of Magnolia Vase by Sandra L. Mollon
Photo courtesy of The National Quilt Museum

You will find bullion knots on the hedgehog, in the dragonfly tail, and alongside the body of the butterfly.

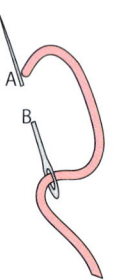

1. Bring the needle up at A and insert back in at B, bringing the tip of the needle back to the front of your fabric near to A. Hold in place there.

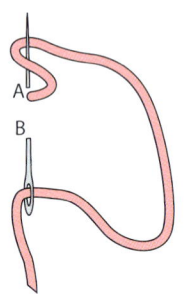

2. Grab the thread at A and wrap it around the tip of the needle as many times as will equal the desired length of the knot (typically 5–7 wraps).

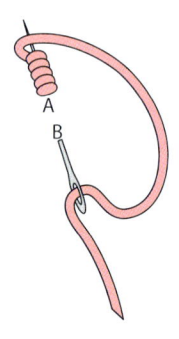

3. Gently pull the needle through the wraps, holding them in place while you do.

36   Seasons of Life Quilt

TECHNIQUES

Buttonhole Stitch

The buttonhole stitch is used as an outline in the wings of the dragonfly and also occasionally in outlining Broderie Perse instead of appliqué.

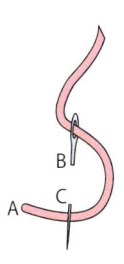

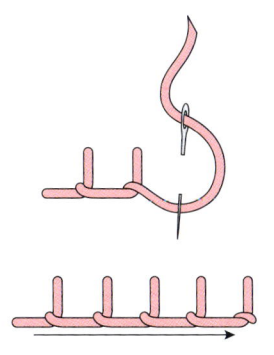

Dragonfly, by Sandra L. Mollon

The wings have small buttonhole stitches in a single strand of variegated cotton floss, stem-stitched legs and wing veins, and backstitched antennae. The body is couched Memory Thread (by DMC) in silver, and the beads were added for the body center, head, and eyes.

1. Coming up at A from the back, insert the needle at B and come back up at C, making sure your needle crosses the thread.

2. Continue this stitch until your outline is complete.

Chain Stitch

The chain stitch is used often as the center vein in large leaves to add a substantial line of embroidery.

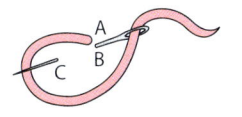

1. Come up from the back at A. Make a small loop while reinserting the needle at B, close to A. Bring the needle up at C, making sure the needle crosses over the loop.

2. Continue stitching, always coming back through the previous loop, until the line is complete.

Detail of the Roses in a Silver Vase blocks by Sandra L. Mollon, showing chain stitches on leaf
Photo courtesy of The National Quilt Museum

Embroidery ❀ 37

Couching

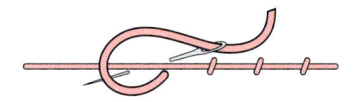

A couching stitch is used to anchor a ribbon or yarn in place. Simply bring your thread up on one side of the yarn or ribbon and down on the opposite, making neat perpendicular stitches.

Featherstitch

Used to embellish the rosebuds, the featherstitch gracefully adds the look of tiny hairs when done in a single fine embroidery thread.

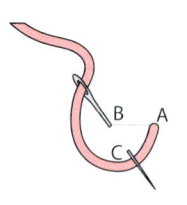

Detail of the Roses in a Silver Vase block by Sandra L. Mollon, showing featherstitches at folded rosebuds
Photo courtesy of The National Quilt Museum

1. Bring the thread from the back at A, down again to the left at B, and up at C, crossing your needle over the thread.

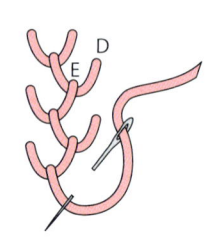

2. On your next stitch, instead of moving to the left, this time swing to the right, alternating left and right until your line is completed.

Fly Stitch

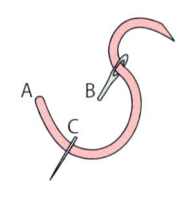

1. Bring the needle up from the back at A. Insert back into your fabric to the right at B, and in one movement, come up at C.

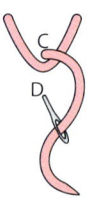

2. Be sure the tip of your needle crosses over your thread. Once that happens, reinsert just below at D.

TIP Several of these stitches stacked on top of each other look lovely on a small appliquéd leaf.

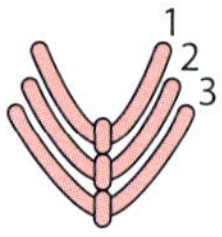

The fly stitch is a great way to dress up a simple leaf, as it gives the appearance of a leaf vein. This appliqué leaf features fly stitch embroidery in size 12 green perle cotton.

This leaf is made from a piece of green Ultrasuede covered completely in embroidery using a fly stitch worked in two strands of variegated cotton floss.

38 ❦ Seasons of Life Quilt

TECHNIQUES

French Knot

Detail of a flower by Jeanette (Heidi) Gorthy, showing both bullion knots and French knots

This stitch forms a small raised knot, as shown in the center of the flower. Surrounding the center French knots are rows of bullion knots.

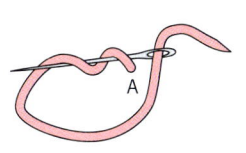

1. Coming up at A from the back, wrap the needle 2–3 times, with the thread close to the fabric.

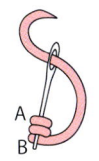

2. Place a finger on this wrap. Reinsert the needle close to A, and bring the thread through the wraps back to the wrong side.

Lazy Daisy Stitch

The lazy daisy stitch is a decorative stitch that can add detail along the side of a leaf or form a small flower in silk ribbon embroidery.

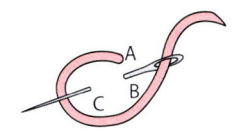

1. Coming up from the back at A, reinsert needle at B and up again at C.

2. The tip of your needle should go over the thread to form a small loop. Bring the needle to the back just behind the loop at D.

3. Pull the thread to the back to complete the stitch.

Ribbon Stitch

The most common stitch in silk ribbon embroidery is the ribbon stitch. You will love how fast and easy it is!

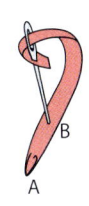

1. Coming up at A, lay your ribbon down against the fabric smoothly. Reinsert the needle through the ribbon at B, at whatever length you want the stitch to be. Generally, I make my stitches about 3/8″ long.

2. Gently pull the ribbon through to the back to form a small point with tiny folds.

TIP Threading Ribbon

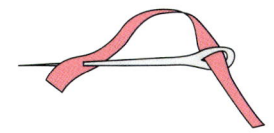

1. To tie silk ribbon onto your needle, insert the ribbon through the eye of your needle, and then pierce the ribbon about an 1/8″ from the end.

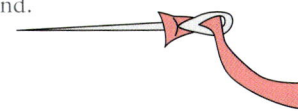

2. Pull the long end of the ribbon back snugly to lock the needle onto the ribbon, making it easier to sew.

Running Stitch

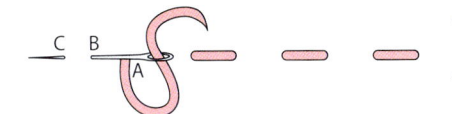

This stitch is often used to gather fabric, ribbon, or trim.

The needle simply moves in and out of the fabric in evenly spaced increments.

Embroidery 39

Satin Stitch

Satin stitches add a continuous smooth area of filled embroidery. They are a series of straight parallel stitches filling in evenly front and back.

1. Secure your thread on the back of your fabric with a few backstitches.

2. Bring the thread to the front and make a series of straight parallel stitches, filling out the area evenly in the front and back, until your shape is filled.

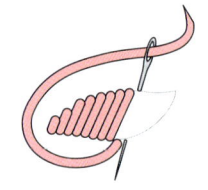

3. End your stitching by backstitching to tie off on the reverse side.

Detail of the Autumn's Bounty block by Sandra L. Mollon. The small acorn has satin stitching on one side, and the eye is surrounded by stem stitching in a single strand of yellow silk floss.
Photo courtesy of The National Quilt Museum

Stem Stitch

This stitch is typically used to outline or draw emphasis to an appliqué. I use it to outline the eyes in my animals and to add veins in leaves or very fine stems.

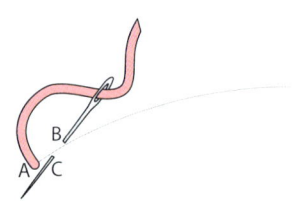

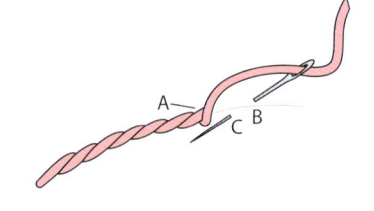

1. Coming up at A, reinsert the needle at B on the drawn line. Bring the tip of the needle back up at C, at a slight angle and close to A.

2. Continue the stitches along the line. The stitches look like the coils in a rope when done correctly.

Detail of the Wild Strawberry Vines Corner block by Sandra L. Mollon. The strawberries have both ribbon stitches and lazy daisy stitches done in 4mm green silk ribbon.
Photo courtesy of The National Quilt Museum

Straight Stitch

A very easy in-and-out stitch, the straight stitch is used to form a short line of embroidery.

40　Seasons of Life Quilt

TECHNIQUES

Using Ink and Colored Pencils on Fabric

Detail of the Magnolia and Doves block by Sandra L. Mollon
Photo courtesy of The National Quilt Museum

All-Purpose Ink (by Tsukineko) is perfect for shading or for adding highlights on fabric. Most colors are transparent, which means they allow for the print and weave of a fabric to show through. The colors that are opaque (more like fabric paint) are White (#80) and the metallics. They completely obscure the fabric unless applied very lightly. Ink doesn't change the hand of the fabric, works on both silk or cotton, and is permanent when heat set. This makes it a great choice for adding depth and realism to your work.

All-Purpose Ink (by Tsukineko)

I apply the inks with Fantastix foam-core applicators (by Tsukineko), which are made specifically for the inks, or with small paint brushes. The Fantastix applicators come in bullet point (blunt) or brush point. I use the bullet-point brushes for blending; they can be rubbed in small circles or lines and are best used for adding subtle shading. Use the brush point to add small dots or finer lines.

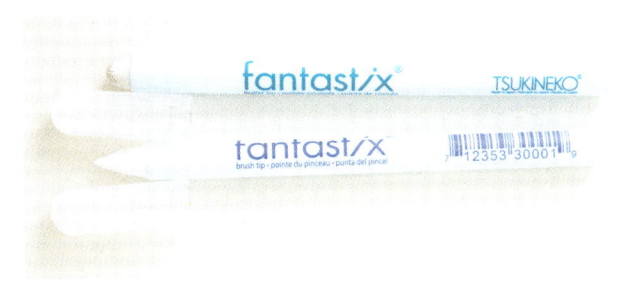

In addition to the small bottles of ink, Tsukineko also makes the ink in marker form for many colors. The colors are the same as the bottles and have coordinating numbers.

Fabrico dual-tip markers (by Tsukineko)

Fantastix bullet-tip and brush-tip applicators (by Tsukineko)

How to Apply Ink

Dip the Fantastix applicator into the bottle, one applicator per color. Rub off excess ink on a scrap cloth. As you do this, notice that the color—dark at first—lightens considerably as you continue to rub. When you get to the shade you like, you can start to color on your appliqué fabric.

I usually press freezer paper to the wrong side of my fabric to support where I want to ink, as the freezer paper holds the fabric smoothly in place while you work. Ink can be added to appliqué shapes that are already prepared for appliqué, with edges turned, or prior to turning as desired.

How to Apply Markers

With both a brush point and a hard fine point, the dual tips give options for adding both shading and fine lines. To use the brush point, simply hold the marker almost horizontally, allowing the side of the brush point to shade the edges of your work.

How to Apply Pens and Colored Pencils

Detail of the Magnolia Vase block by Sandra L. Mollon, showing fine detail lines done with a Pigma Micron pen and subtle shading under the lines with colored pencils
Photo courtesy of The National Quilt Museum

I also use brown or black Pigma Micron pens for very fine-detail lines in sizes 01–05.

Colored pencils are also a great way to add color or subtle shading on fabric. Use them directly on your fabric and heat set with a dry iron. Purchase the highest-quality colored pencils that you can afford—better pencils have more pigment and have an oil core rather than wax, which makes them easier to use on fabric.

Gallery of Quilts

Seasons of Life; 76″ × 76″; appliquéd, pieced, and hand quilted by Barbara Neumayer, 2017

Flora and Fauna, 85″ × 85″, pieced by Linda Perricone, quilted by Lora Zmak, 2017

44   Seasons of Life Quilt

Seasons of Life, 88″ × 88″, pieced by Jeanette (Heidi) Gorthy, quilted by Laurie Grant, 2018

Gallery of Quilts ❖ 45

Seasons of Life, 64″ × 76″, pieced by Tina McConnell, quilted by Dianne Schweickert, 2019

46 Seasons of Life Quilt

Flora, Fauna, Butterflies, and Bugs, 53″ × 53″, pieced by Beth Butura, quilted by Dianne Schweickert, 2018
Some blocks are from the *Baltimore Album and Beyond* books by Elly Sienkiewicz (from C&T Publishing).

Gallery of Quilts 47

Magnolia and Doves block, pieced by Jollyne Toste

48　Seasons of Life Quilt

Remembering Mary, 88″ × 89″, pieced by Judy Green, machine quilted by Darla Padilla of Wildflower Quilting, 2019

Gallery of Quilts   49

Planning the Project:
Seasons of Life

Seasons of Life, by Sandra L. Mollon

Photo courtesy of The National Quilt Museum

Layout Diagram

Finished quilt: 88½″ × 88½″

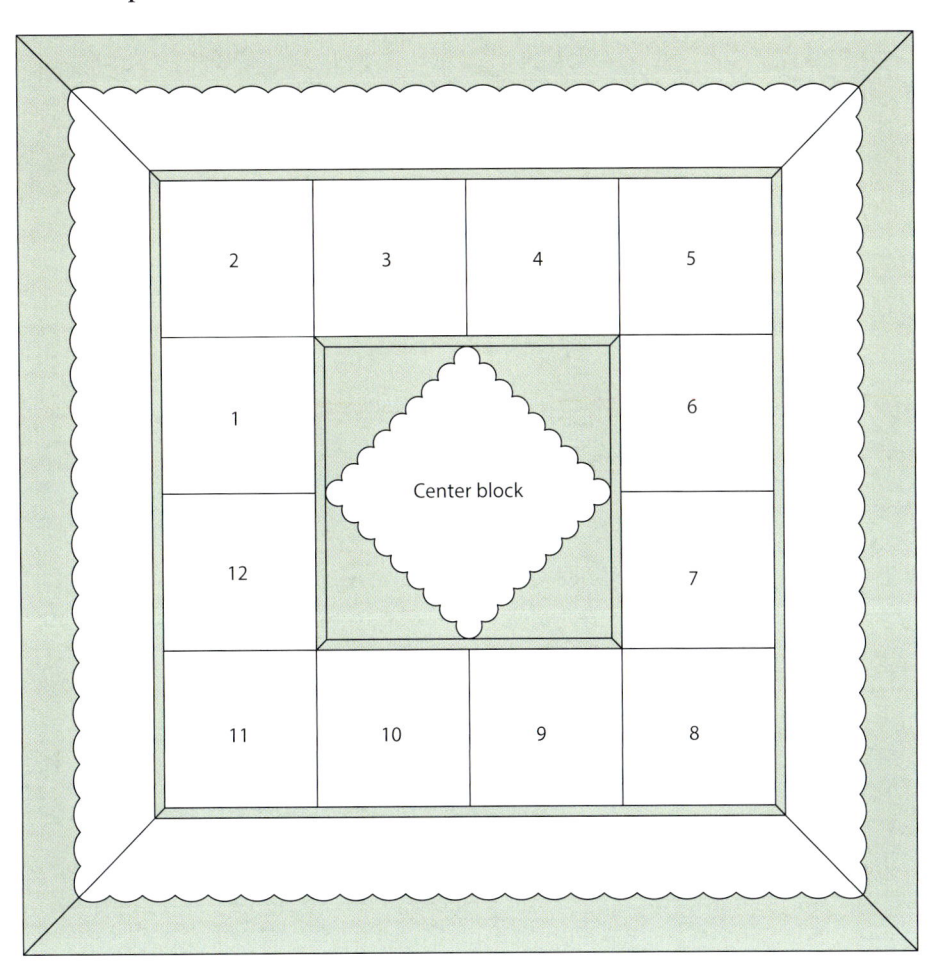

BLOCK PLACEMENT

Spring Blocks

1. Peony Vase
2. Wild Strawberry Vines Corner
3. Among the Foxgloves

Summer Blocks

4. Roses in a Silver Vase
5. Blackberry Corner
6. Magnolia Vase

Fall Blocks

7. Autumn's Bounty
8. Oak and Acorn Corner
9. Hedgehog in the Garden

Winter Blocks

10. Magnolia and Doves
11. Arts and Crafts Poinsettia Corner
12. Circle of Roses

Center Block

Ruched Rose in a Crown of Flowers

Preparing the Appliqué Block Patterns

Prepare full-size working appliqué patterns on paper. The quadrant patterns for each block are found within the instructions for each block. The center block and border patterns are found on the pullout. Having full-size, properly aligned working patterns is essential. Use them for your final placement onto the background fabric. You will need a lightbox to trace the patterns.

1. For the blocks, cut a 15″ × 15″ square of paper and fold neatly, creasing the paper in half top to bottom and then in half again right to left. This will result in a square of paper with 4 quadrants.

2. The 4 corner blocks are symmetrical, so you only need 1 quadrant pattern for each. This is a 3-step process.

- Trace the pattern onto the prepared (creased) paper in one corner, aligning the centers.
- Fold the paper in half and trace through it onto the adjacent side, using a lightbox to create the reversed or mirror image.
- Open that half, fold the paper in half again, and trace the first 2 sides to make the full pattern.

3. The remaining blocks have 4 separate quadrant patterns. Trace each pattern onto the appropriate quadrant on the prepared paper, aligning the centers.

52   Seasons of Life Quilt

Cutting the Block Backgrounds

The block backgrounds are cut 16″ × 16″ and will be trimmed to 15½″ × 15½″ after the appliqué is complete.

12″						
16″ × 16″	16″ × 16″	16″ × 16″	16″ × 16″	16″ × 16″	16″ × 16″	
16″ × 16″	16″ × 16″	16″ × 16″	16″ × 16″	16″ × 16″	16″ × 16″	21″ × 21″

1. If the fabric is at least 44″ wide, cut 1 long strip approximately 12″ wide along the length of the yardage and save that piece for some of the border pieces.

2. The remaining 32″ width of the yardage is wide enough to cut 2 blocks side by side. Cut all 12 blocks, at least 16″ × 16″, this way.

3. Cut a 21″ × 21″ square for the center block.

4. Set aside the remaining fabric, along with the 12″ strip, for the accent strips and borders.

TIP 🌿 Don't trim away the selvage until you are ready to trim the blocks before you sew them together. The selvage helps minimize raveling.

Appliqué is traditionally done on backgrounds cut slightly larger than the required size for piecing to make the quilt top. This makes a lot of sense. Appliqué can sometimes take up or shrink the background square slightly (usually ⅛″ or less) just due to the sewing itself. While this is normal and to be expected as you sew, having oversized block backgrounds helps you avoid skimpy piecing seams. Also, fraying sometimes occurs, and you want a clean-cut edge when you are ready to join your blocks together.

TIP 🌿 If you decide to use silk as your background fabric, cut the backgrounds larger than the 16″ × 16″ square as I recommended above for cotton. Since many silk dupioni fabrics are 54″ wide off the bolt, you have ample room to cut the squares at least 17½″ × 17½″, so that you may serge or stitch the edges to prevent fray while you work.

Block Patterns and Instructions

Refer to How to Master Prepared-Edge Appliqué (page 21) for how to create the templates, how to cut the fabric for the appliqués, how to lay out the appliqués for each block, and how to glue and sew the appliqués to the block background fabric.

Once you have appliquéd the block, refer to the following embellishment suggestions.

Detail of *Seasons of Life*, by Sandra L. Mollon
Photo courtesy of The National Quilt Museum

Spring

Block 1: Peony Vase

Peony Vase block, by Sandra L. Mollon
Photo courtesy of The National Quilt Museum

This block features a variety of silk or cotton fabrics in pinks for the peony petals, a golden-yellow center filled with embroidery stitches, a silver-gray vase with darker gray footings, and various green leaves. Start the block by adding the vase and footings. Add the leaves and then make the flowers. I like to make all my flower petals, remove the freezer paper, and then "glue assemble" them together using the master pattern. Once the flower units are glued together, simply position them on the block and complete the appliqué stitches.

Detail of Peony Vase block by Sandra L. Mollon
Photo courtesy of The National Quilt Museum

Embroidery details in this block include the chain stitch in green for the large veins in leaves, the stem stitch in green for smaller veins as desired, rows of bullion knots in yellow around the edges of the peony flower centers, and French knots in yellow in the very center of the peony flower centers.

Peony Vase
Upper left quadrant

Center

56　Seasons of Life Quilt

SEASONS OF LIFE

Peony Vase
Upper right quadrant

Center

Block Patterns and Instructions **57**

Center

Peony Vase
Lower left quadrant

58   Seasons of Life Quilt

SEASONS OF LIFE

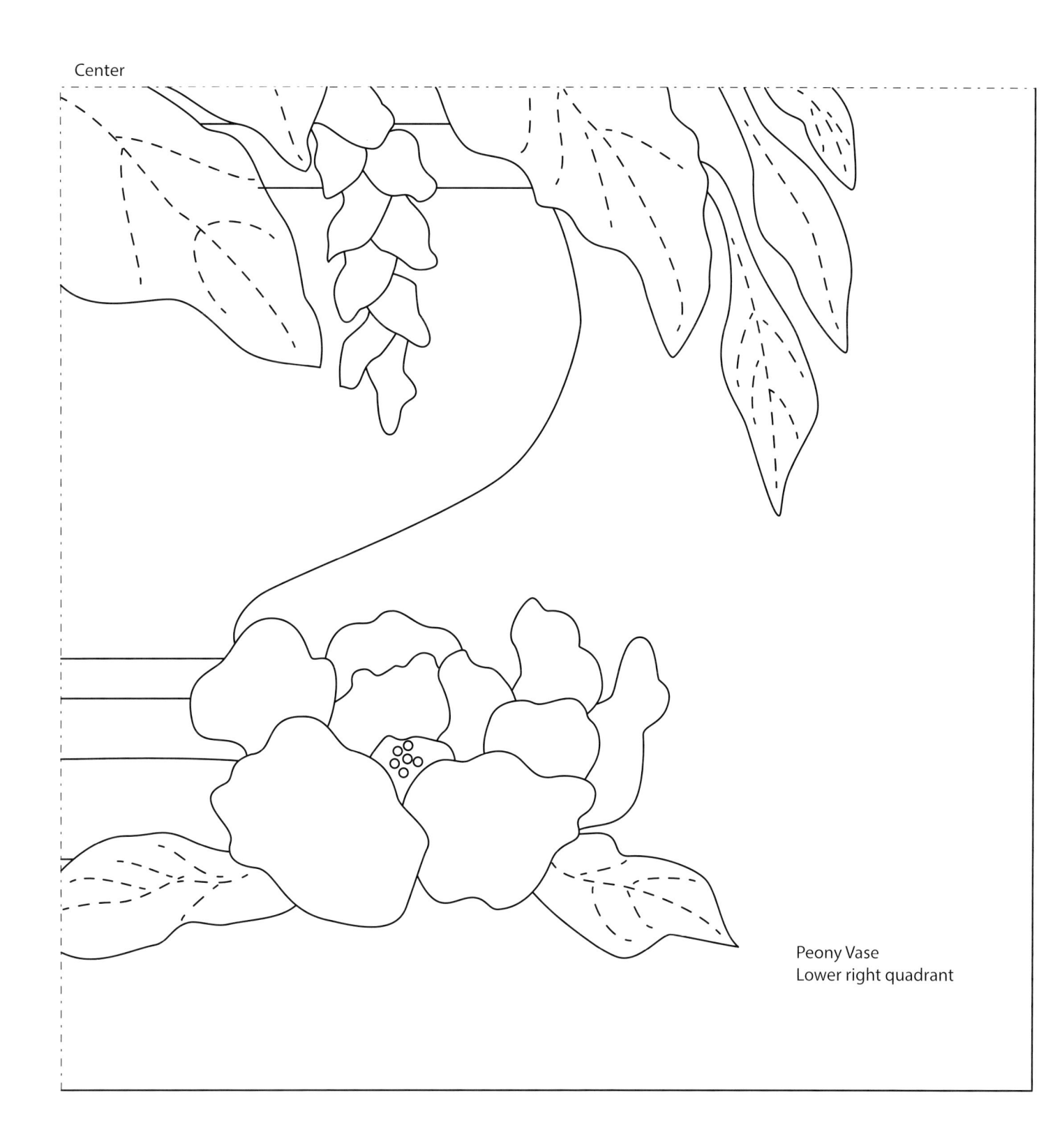

Center

Peony Vase
Lower right quadrant

Block Patterns and Instructions   **59**

Block 2: Wild Strawberry Vines Corner

Wild Strawberry Vines Corner block, by Sandra L. Mollon
Photo courtesy of The National Quilt Museum

This block is inspired by the symmetrical designs of the Arts And Crafts Movement of the early 1900s. It was important to the quilt's design that I position a block with an X shape in the 4 corners, as X shapes help draw the eyes back to the center. I used a variety of green colors, and I also varied the reds used for the strawberries to add interest. Begin the block with the 4 center pieces; then add your stems, leaves, berries, and yo-yo flowers.

Detail of Wild Strawberry Vines Corner block by Sandra L. Mollon
Photo courtesy of The National Quilt Museum

Details of this block include beading on the strawberries. I generally use small dark-red beads; however, green beads are another great option because they resemble the seeds on strawberries.

Additionally, I made yo-yo flowers for the blossoms that tie the center of the block to the vine. The block pattern shows just 2 flowers, but my student Heidi Gorthy made 3 in each corner, and they look lovely. You might consider adding French knots in yellow ribbon or floss for the centers of the blossoms.

Add a stem stitch in dark green for the small vines on the dashed lines. Add either a ribbon stitch or a lazy daisy stitch in 4mm-wide silk ribbon in medium green for the small leaves on top of the berries. The dashed lines inside the leaves can be quilted in or added with a stem stitch.

SEASONS OF LIFE

Wild Strawberry Vines Corner
Block quadrant

Center

Block Patterns and Instructions 61

Block 3: Among the Foxgloves

Among the Foxgloves block, by Sandra L. Mollon
Photo courtesy of The National Quilt Museum

Detail of Among the Foxgloves block by Sandra L. Mollon
Photo courtesy of The National Quilt Museum

To appliqué, first complete the flowers, bunny, leaves, and stems in fabric. For the bunny body, use a single piece of light beige silk, if desired. The curve of the leg and under the arm are added with quilting lines later. Use a small piece of black Ultrasuede for the eye shape and add a small dot of White (#80) All-Purpose Ink to highlight. The ear folds are light pink fabric. The leaves can be made from a silk crepe, as I did here, or in 2 shades of green cotton fabric.

This block has inked foxglove flowers; beaded berries; silk ribbon embroidery; and, of course, a beaded, embroidered, and inked dragonfly.

Inking details also include small, random tan dots on the inside of the foxgloves with a Sand (#152) Fabrico marker and slightly darkened centers using a Truffle (#155) Fabrico marker. I lightly brushed on White (#80) All-Purpose Ink between the dots with a Fantastix (brush point).

62   Seasons of Life Quilt

Embroider the small stems on the dashed lines in a light sage-green floss for the berry stems and a variegated pink/green 7mm silk ribbon in a ribbon stitch for the leaves. After the quilting is complete, add the beaded berries at the top of the stems and a darker green 4mm silk ribbon for the leaves on top of the berries. The larger leaves on the left side can be embroidered with a chain stitch or stem stitch down the center on the dashed line. Embroider the fine lines of the flower at the top with 2 strands of a purple/red embroidery floss, and add little flowers at the end with 4mm silk ribbon in a matching color using a ribbon stitch.

Add silk ribbon embroidery details to the top of the foxglove flower stem. To get the look of the small buds and leaves that occur on those stems, add French knots in purple 7mm silk ribbon at intervals, and then add green 4mm or 7mm silk ribbon leaves with a ribbon stitch.

For the dragonfly, lightly trace the shape of the wings, legs, and antennae *only* onto your background fabric with a fine 01 Pigma Micron pen. Heat set by pressing with a hot iron for 10 seconds; then brush on Champagne Mist (#74) All-Purpose Ink inside the wings for a very light metallic sheen. If you wish for blue-green metallic wings, simply mix a small drop of Champagne Mist All-Purpose Ink with a drop of Celadon (#60) All-Purpose Ink.

For the embroidery, use a single strand of brown floss to stem stitch the veins in the wings, the legs, and the antennae. Using variegated cotton floss (single strand), stitch a tiny 1/8″ buttonhole stitch to outline the wings. Use a single strand of matching floss to couch on a 6″ length of Memory Thread or gimp that has first been coiled at one end and folded back on itself with a small round gap forming below the coil, hiding the other end back under the coil.

Add bullion knots over the tail at random intervals. Stitch French knots (or beads) to fill the body center with a variegated blue-and-gray floss, single or double strands. Add a bead for the head and 2 smaller beads for the eyes if desired.

TIP Optionally, you may wish to find a printed butterfly fabric, cut out a butterfly of your choice, and appliqué it in place instead, as described for The Bee (page 81).

Among the Foxgloves
Upper left quadrant

Center

64 Seasons of Life Quilt

SEASONS OF LIFE

Among the Foxgloves
Upper right quadrant

Center

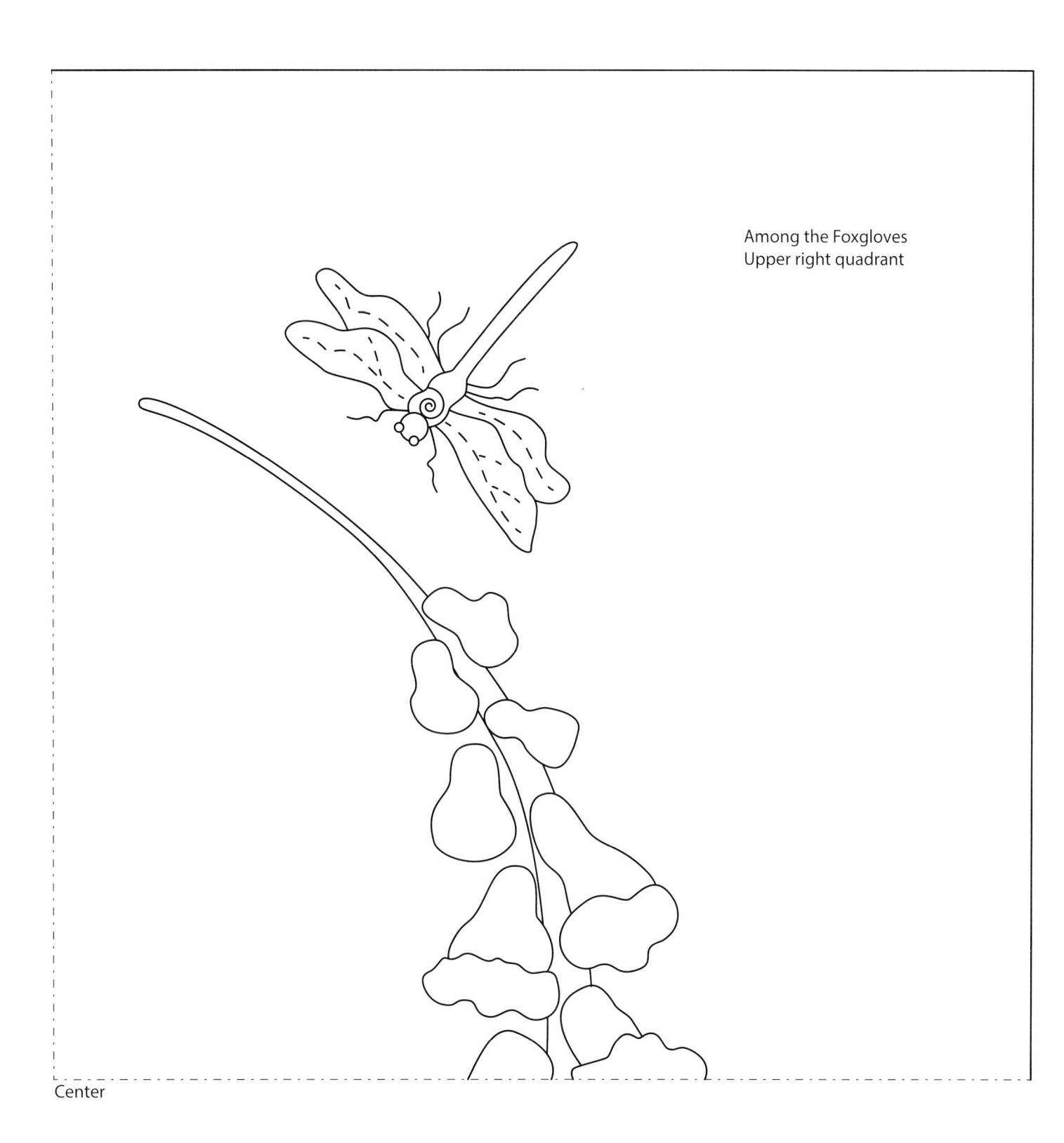

Block Patterns and Instructions **65**

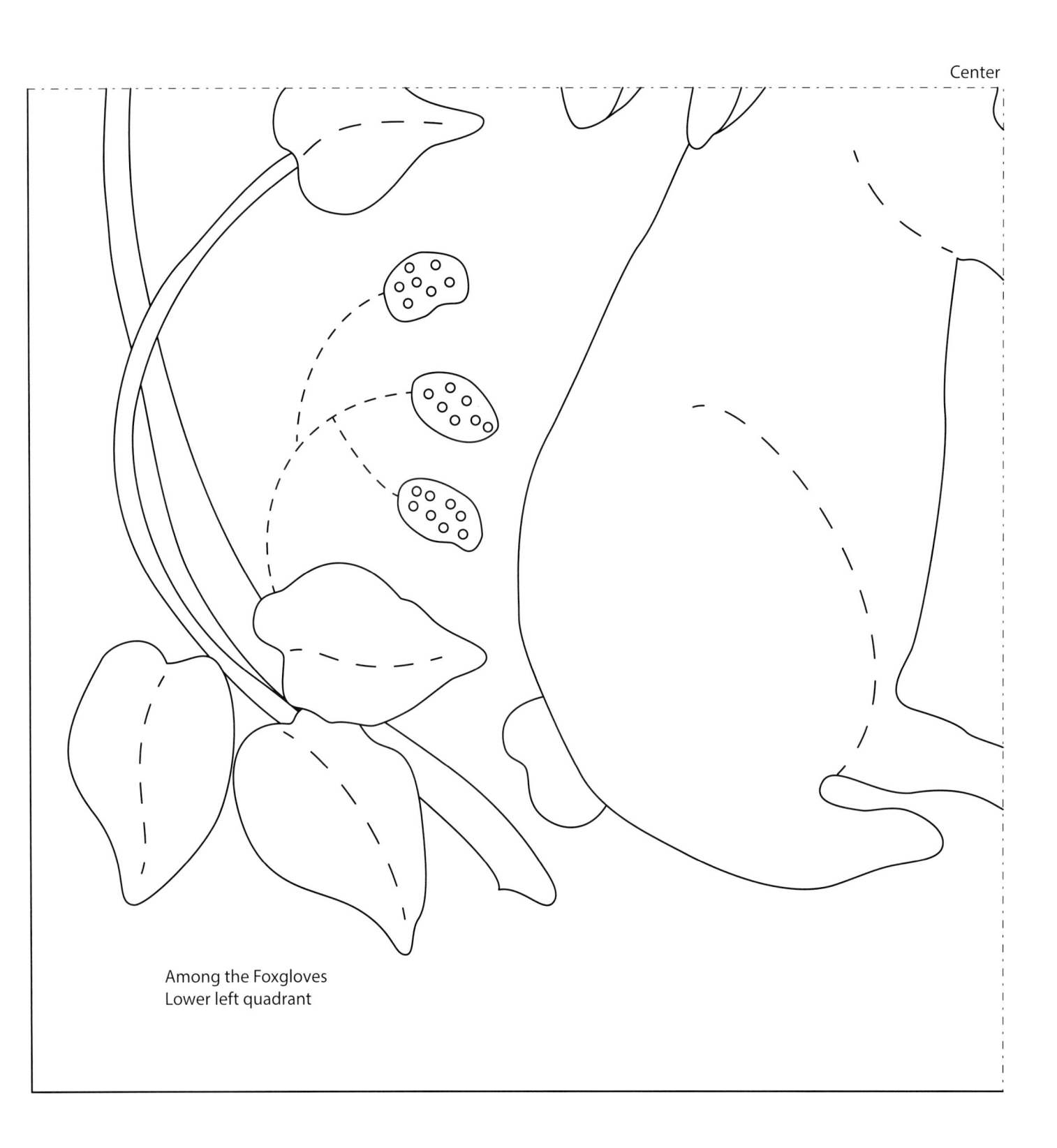

Center

Among the Foxgloves
Lower left quadrant

SEASONS OF LIFE

Center

Among the Foxgloves
Lower right quadrant

Block Patterns and Instructions **67**

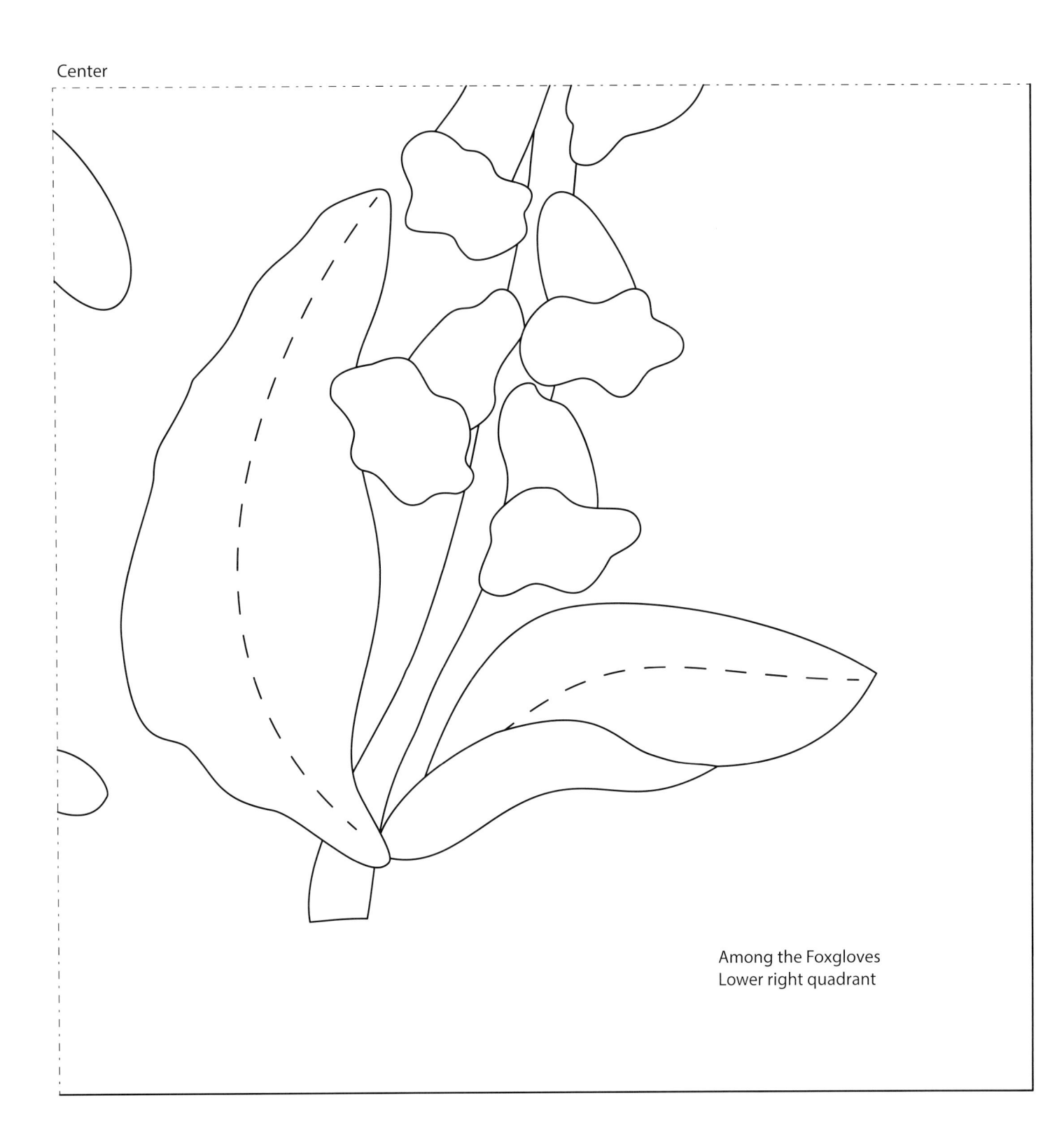

Summer

Block 4: Roses in a Silver Vase

Roses in a Silver Vase block, by Sandra L. Mollon
Photo courtesy of The National Quilt Museum

Detail of Roses in a Silver Vase block by Sandra L. Mollon
Photo courtesy of The National Quilt Museum

This block was worked with a silver silk dupioni fabric and has darker-gray silk footing and handles. You may wish to use a silver-colored cotton fabric. I recommend using Ultrasuede for the handles. Stitch a narrow ribbon (¼″ wide) or strip of fabric around the narrow part of the vase. I glue basted another piece of fabric behind the teardrop shapes and then appliquéd the turned edges down to hold them in place.

Embroidery details in this block include a chain stitch for the leaf center veins and a stem stitch for the small leaf veins, worked in greens with a single or double strand of floss as desired. Use a single strand of a medium-green silk or cotton floss in a featherstitch for the rose hairs. Of course, the buds are folded rosebuds. I added a circle of satin stitching to the butterfly, a satin-stitched abdomen with 2 bullion knots on both sides, and antennae in a stem stitch. I worked it all in brown with a single strand of floss. Add a French knot for the head, if desired, or a small bead.

SEASONS OF LIFE

Roses in a Silver Vase
Upper left quadrant

Center

Block Patterns and Instructions   **69**

Roses in a Silver Vase
Upper right quadrant

Center

70 Seasons of Life Quilt

SEASONS OF LIFE

Center

Roses in a Silver Vase
Lower left quadrant

Block Patterns and Instructions   71

Center

Roses in a Silver Vase
Lower right quadrant

72   Seasons of Life Quilt

Block 5: Blackberry Corner

Blackberry Corner block, by Jeanette Heidi Gorthy

This is perhaps my personal favorite of all of the blocks in this quilt. Details include using a variety of greens for the leaves. I generally used dark greens for the center leaves and medium to lighter greens for the remainder. I tucked a small beige ½″ finished yo-yo in the center, and the stems were cut from brown and tan Ultrasuede, so they were easier to make.

Detail of Blackberry Corner block by Sandra L. Mollon
Photo courtesy of The National Quilt Museum

Embroider the fine lines with a stem stitch in brown floss; I recommend 2 strands. The flowers are pink petals with a yellow center. Add a few French knots in yellow and bullion knots, also in yellow cotton or silk floss, to the center of the flowers. Bead the berries on felt in dark plums and reds, with some berries getting ivory and pinker beads (all size 8, generally) to represent unripe berries. Sew the berries in place after the quilting is complete. The detail lines in the leaves were added with quilting stitches.

Blackberry Corner
Block quadrant

Center

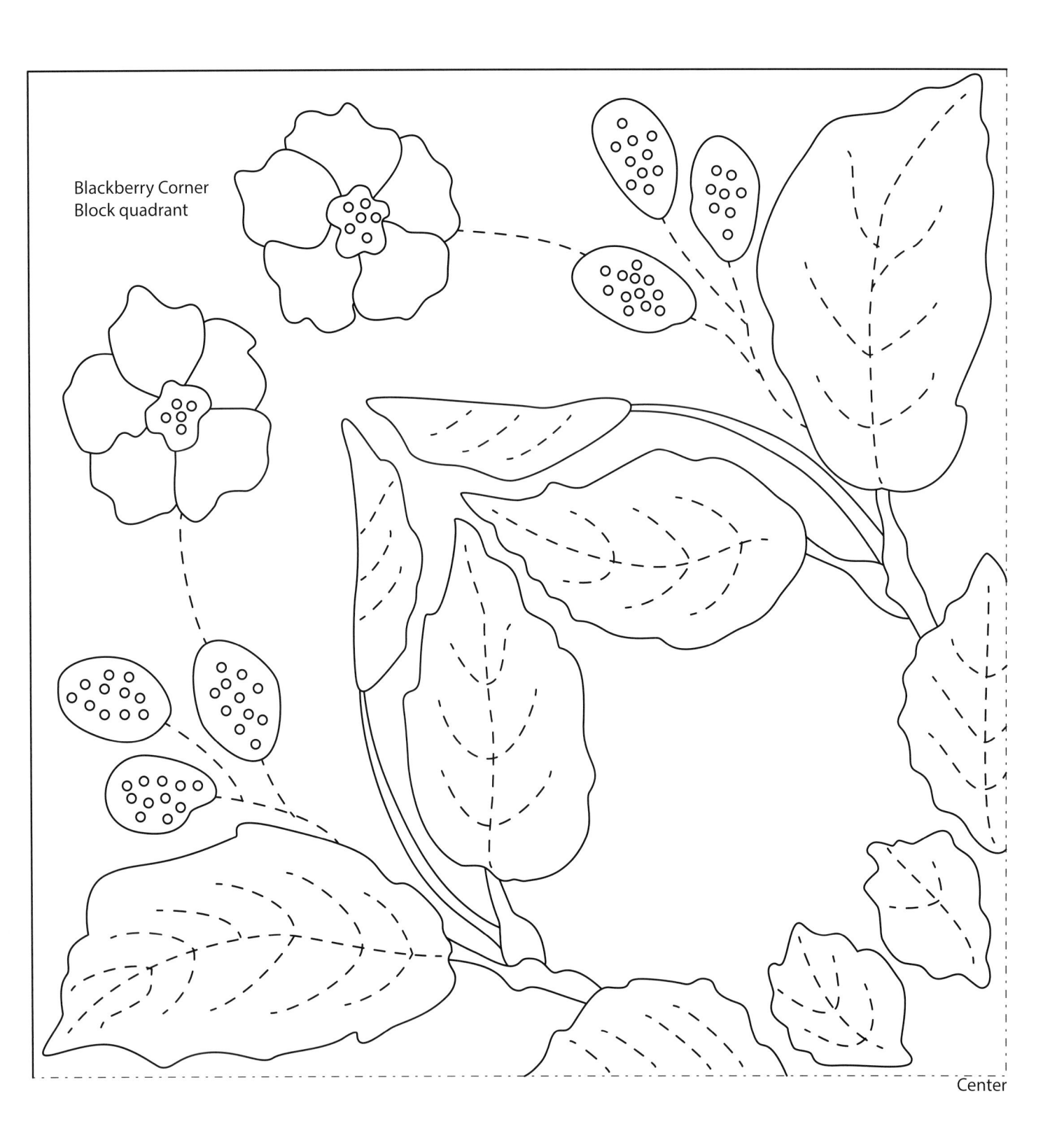

74 Seasons of Life Quilt

Block 6: Magnolia Vase

Magnolia Vase block, by Sandra L. Mollon
Photo courtesy of The National Quilt Museum

Detail of Magnolia Vase block by Sandra L. Mollon
Photo courtesy of The National Quilt Museum

A good place to start with this block is to appliqué the vase first. Once that is in place, you can do the vines and small flowers. Use the glue-assembly technique to put your roses together, and then add your embellishments.

There are a few fun details I added to this block, like the frayed strip of fabric behind the yo-yo in the light purple flower's center (see Yo-Yos and Yo-Yo Flowers, page 28). The magnolia and other flower centers are also embellished with embroidery and beading. Surround the center of the magnolia flower with rows of bullion knots and hide the edge of the appliquéd pink/yellow silk. Then add yellow beads for more texture. Add beaded berries to a stem on the right, done in deep-purple size 8 beads.

Magnolia Vase
Upper left quadrant

Center

76   Seasons of Life Quilt

SEASONS OF LIFE

Magnolia Vase
Upper right quadrant

Center

Block Patterns and Instructions 77

Center

Magnolia Vase
Lower left quadrant

78 Seasons of Life Quilt

SEASONS OF LIFE

Center

Magnolia Vase
Lower right quadrant

Block Patterns and Instructions 79

Fall

Block 7: Autumn's Bounty

Autumn's Bounty block, by Sandra L. Mollon
Photo courtesy of The National Quilt Museum

Detail of Autumn's Bounty block by Sandra L. Mollon
Photo courtesy of The National Quilt Museum

To make this block, start by appliquéing the stems, branches, and leaves. The squirrel sits on a leaf and hides the ends of the branches. I added a layer of light stuffing to the squirrel body and a short length of yarn couched in place on the tail. See the details listed at right and on the next page to add those.

Be sure to complete the appliqué prior to adding your embroidery details!

The dashed lines indicate where you might wish to add embroidery. Use a chain stitch with 2 strands of floss or a single strand of perle cotton, size 12, for the central vein on the leaves. The smaller lines coming off the center vein are embroidered in a stem stitch using a single strand. You may consider using a single color or a variegated floss in greens and golds.

The acorn tops and bottoms were made from brown Ultrasuede. Add French knots with a lighter brown floss, double stranded, on the tops for texture. Then add a satin stitch (single or double stranded) to one-half of each acorn bottom, on top of the Ultrasuede, in a lighter shade of brown or beige to highlight.

80 Seasons of Life Quilt

Lightly stuff the squirrel body with a piece of silk batting, cut ⅛″ smaller than the appliqué shape. Pin or glue baste in place and appliqué, leaving a gap for the yarn on the tail.

To add the couched yarn for the tail, cut a 6″ length of eyelash yarn. Fold it in half, with the fold at the top of the tail and the ends tucked under the body. Pin in place and use a couching stitch, with stitches spaced about ¼″ apart to secure in place. Add some short straight stitches in light brown floss, single strand, to indicate the toes on the foot.

The eye is a small dark brown piece of Ultrasuede. Appliqué it in place and then embroider around it in a stem stitch using a single strand of light gold or medium yellow floss. Add a small dot of White (#80) All-Purpose Ink for the eye highlight. *Note:* It may be necessary to add a second coat of the white ink once the first coat is dry on the dark Ultrasuede.

THE BEE

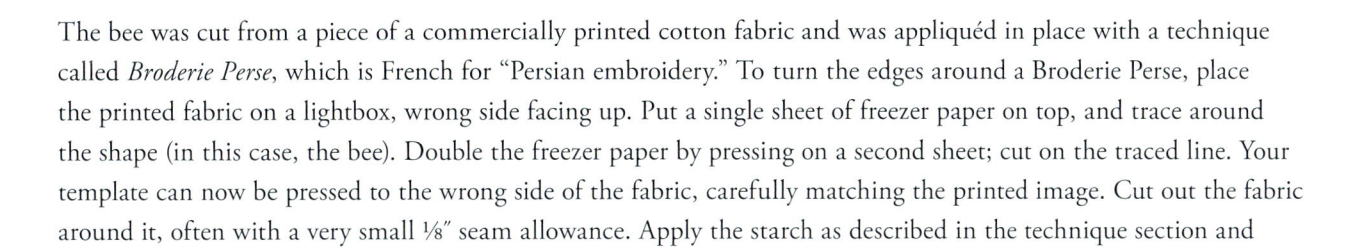

The bee was cut from a piece of a commercially printed cotton fabric and was appliquéd in place with a technique called *Broderie Perse*, which is French for "Persian embroidery." To turn the edges around a Broderie Perse, place the printed fabric on a lightbox, wrong side facing up. Put a single sheet of freezer paper on top, and trace around the shape (in this case, the bee). Double the freezer paper by pressing on a second sheet; cut on the traced line. Your template can now be pressed to the wrong side of the fabric, carefully matching the printed image. Cut out the fabric around it, often with a very small ⅛″ seam allowance. Apply the starch as described in the technique section and turn the edges back, pressing in place. Remove the freezer paper, and it is ready to appliqué into place on your block!

Autumn's Bounty
Upper left quadrant

Center

82 Seasons of Life Quilt

SEASONS OF LIFE

Autumn's Bounty
Upper right quadrant

Center

Block Patterns and Instructions **83**

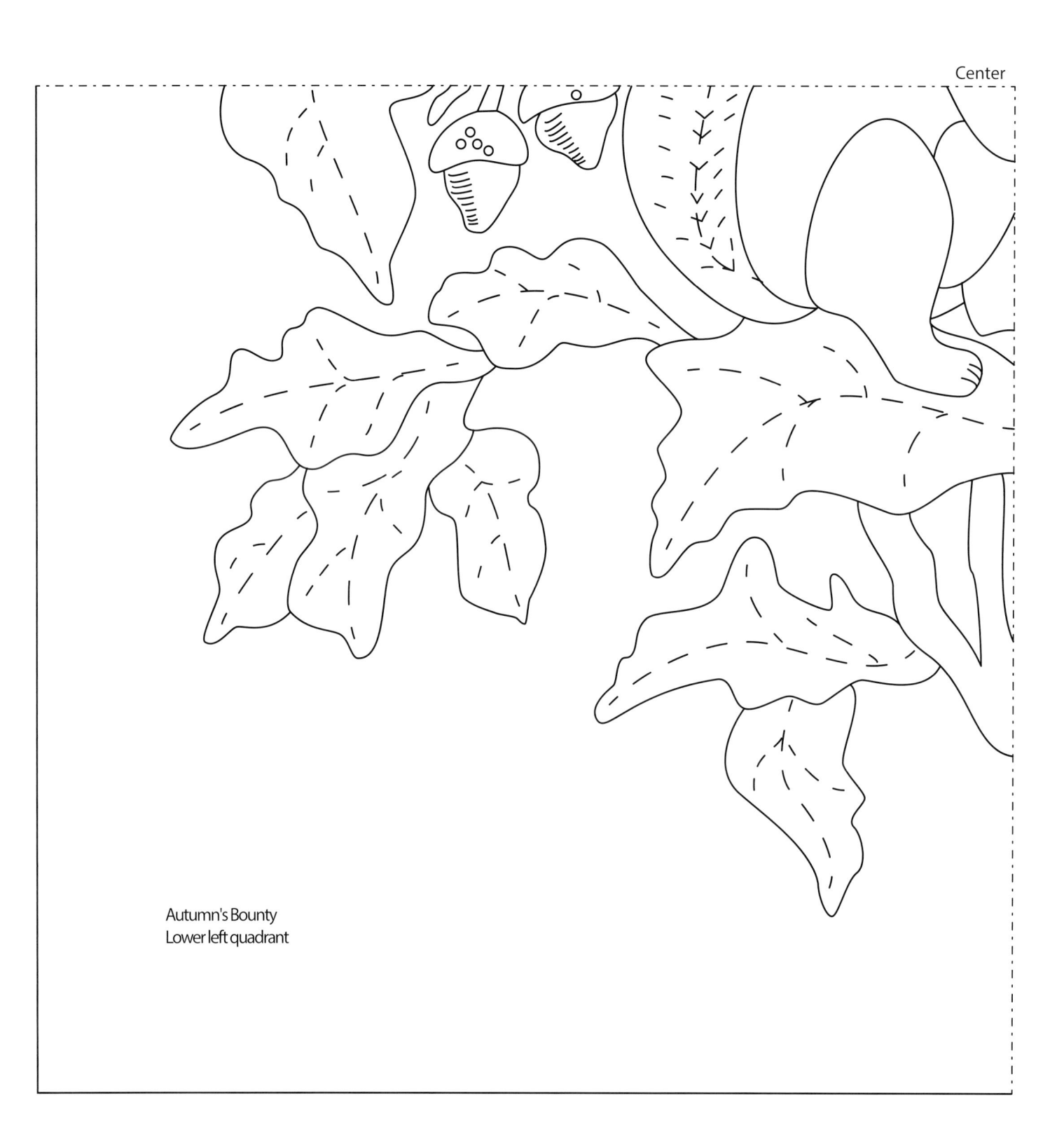

Center

Autumn's Bounty
Lower left quadrant

84   Seasons of Life Quilt

SEASONS OF LIFE

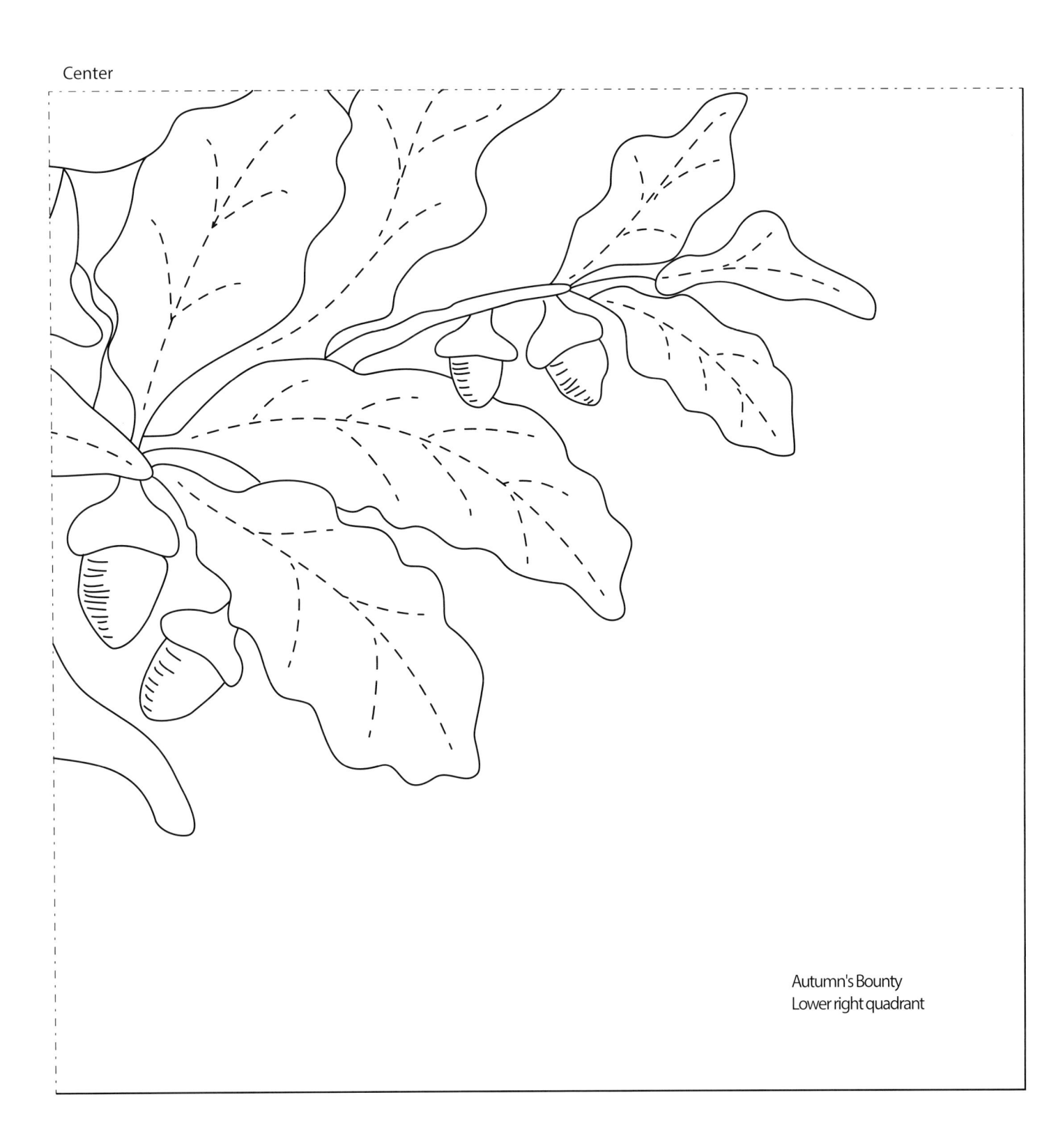

Center

Autumn's Bounty
Lower right quadrant

Block Patterns and Instructions **85**

Block 8: Oak and Acorn Corner

Oak and Acorn Corner block, by Jeanette (Heidi) Gorthy

This simple block is mostly appliqué, with some embroidery details.

Detail of Oak and Acorn Corner block by Sandra L. Mollon

Photo courtesy of The National Quilt Museum

Embroider chain stitches on the center veins of the leaves in 2-stranded cotton floss or size 12 perle cotton. Smaller veins are stem stitched with a single or double strand of cotton floss. I recommend Ultrasuede for the acorn caps. My student Jeanette (Heidi) Gorthy added a small rickrack rose to the center of her block, as seen above.

Seasons of Life Quilt

SEASONS OF LIFE

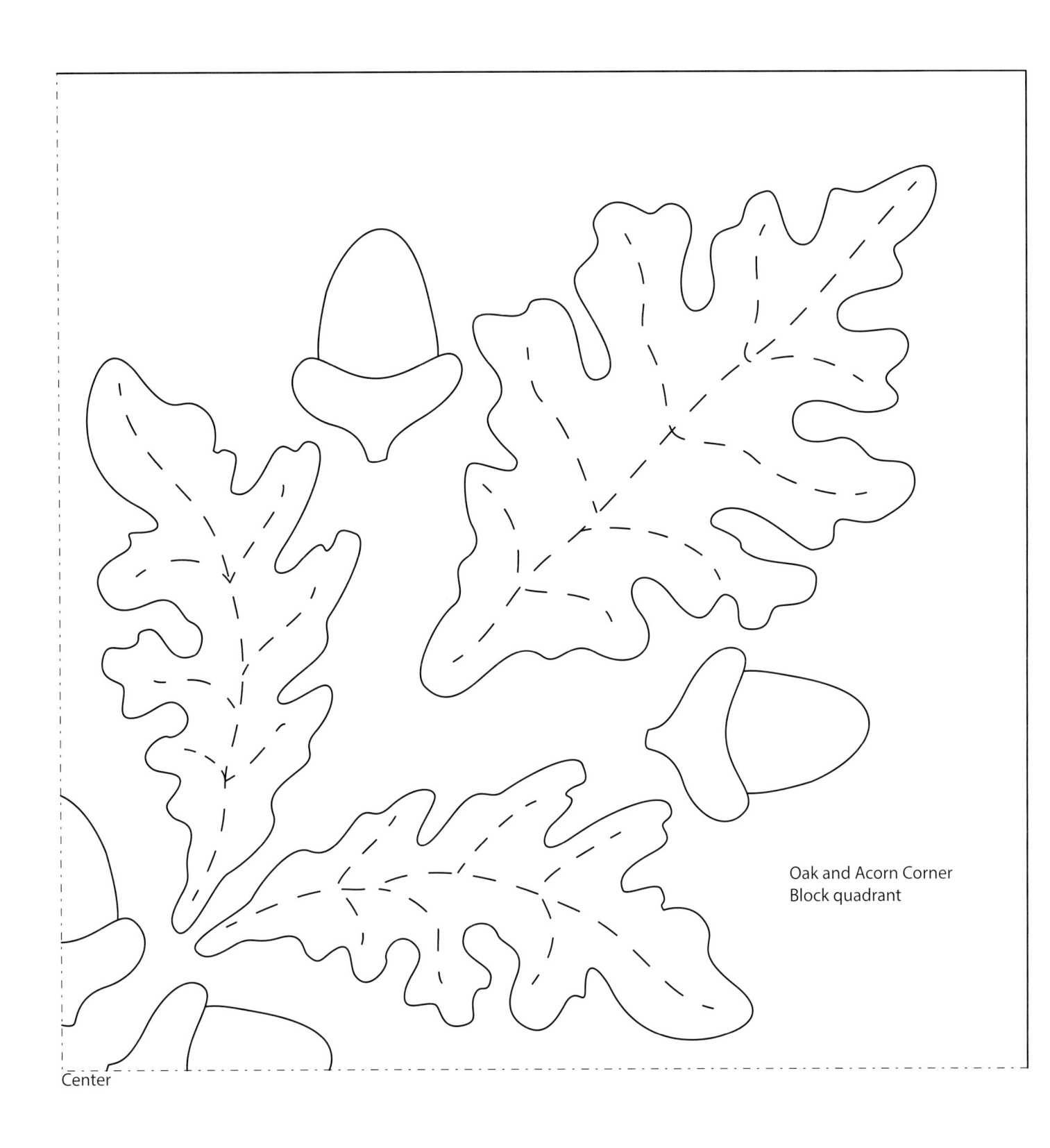

Oak and Acorn Corner
Block quadrant

Center

Block Patterns and Instructions **87**

Block 9: Hedgehog in the Garden

Hedgehog in the Garden block, by Sandra L. Mollon
Photo courtesy of The National Quilt Museum

This charming block has lots of details in both silk ribbon and embroidery added to the appliqué. I do recommend completing all appliqué prior to adding the embellishments.

To begin, make narrow stems for the wheat stalks and vines from a light-brown batik cotton or Ultrasuede, about ⅛" wide. The dark brown stem of the vine on the right side was made from Ultrasuede.

Next, add the leaves from a variety of green fabrics. Once they are appliquéd in place, you can embroider the center veins with a double-stranded cotton floss in a chain stitch or stem stitch.

Each of the small berries to either side of the hedgehog were appliquéd with small circles of reds and pinks, and then embellished with a small bead or French knot in floss. The 3 capped berries have an X embroidered on them with a straight stitch using single-stranded cotton floss.

Add stem stitches in a light brown floss for the fine lines near the top of the wheat stalks and above the wheat seeds. Then add 7mm silk ribbon in a variegated or golden brown ribbon stitch to denote the wheat heads.

Detail of spiderweb by Sandra L. Mollon
Photo courtesy of The National Quilt Museum

Trace the fine lines of the spiderweb with a fine 005 Pigma Micron pen. Embroider with a single strand of a metallic silver thread or a silver floss in a stem stitch or backstitch.

Detail of Hedgehog in the Garden block by Sandra L. Mollon
Photo courtesy of The National Quilt Museum

I made the hedgehog with a medium brown fabric for his back and tan or ecru fabric for the face and stomach area. I shaded the area below the nose with a Fabrico Marker in Sand (#152), with a small amount of Truffle (#155) in the center to give dimension. Ink the fabric to shade it prior to adding the embroidery. Shading the fabric helps you to choose the color of embroidery floss that best matches the color of the shaded area. For inking, add some small nostrils on the nose by darkening with a brown or black 01 Pigma Micron pen on both sides. Then lightly brush on a smudge of White (#80) All-Purpose Ink on top for a highlight.

To embellish, add small circles of black Ultrasuede for the eyes and stitch them in place. Add a small dot of the White (#80) All-Purpose Ink in both eyes. The nose, ears, and feet are all brown or tan Ultrasuede. Once the appliqué is complete, you can add the embroidery.

Use a small embroidery hoop (4″–5″) to stabilize the fabric as you work. The body is covered in a combination of straight stitches and bullion knots in shades of brown, tan, rusty brown, and ecru using single-stranded cotton floss. The direction of the stitches is important, as it gives the appearance of how the fur would lie. Start near the top of the nose in small, short straight stitches, and work outwards. Optionally, you can use a variegated floss in similar color ranges for the stitches on his back.

Hedgehog in the Garden
Upper left quadrant

Center

90   Seasons of Life Quilt

SEASONS OF LIFE

Hedgehog in the Garden
Upper right quadrant

Center

Block Patterns and Instructions 91

Center

Hedgehog in the Garden
Lower left quadrant

92 Seasons of Life Quilt

SEASONS OF LIFE

Center

Hedgehog in the Garden
Lower right quadrant

Block Patterns and Instructions 93

Winter

Block 10: Magnolia and Doves

Magnolia and Doves block, by Sandra L. Mollon
Photo courtesy of The National Quilt Museum

This lovely block symbolizes the season of winter and the winter holidays. The holly, mistletoe, wild roses, and a stately magnolia are all symbolic, and of course the doves stand for peace.

Start your work with the vase. I used a lovely teal jacquard silk and trim in a darker teal Ultrasuede. The stems are brown Ultrasuede; the finer stems were embroidered using a stem stitch in double-stranded cotton floss. Trace the holly berries onto your background fabric using a fine 01 Pigma Micron pen, and then satin stitch with red silk or cotton floss, single or double stranded. To finish, add a small size 08 light green bead. The holly leaves are embroidered with a stem stitch or backstitch in a medium green floss. Optionally, your leaves may have only quilting lines to suggest veins.

To make the body of the doves, I recommend shading them around the bottom with a light brown, rust, or taupe colored pencil. To shade on your off-white fabric, press a piece of freezer paper on the wrong side of the fabric to stabilize it, and color the fabric by smoothly drawing in a circular movement. Blend the colored pencil with your fingertip and heat set with a hot iron.

The body of the doves can be also be padded with a layer of silk batting, inserted prior to appliqué. Always cut the batting a ⅛" smaller than the fabric, pin in place, and then complete your stitching. Add the layers of soft gray and taupe fabrics for the wings. I used a textured taupe interior-decorator fabric for the upper part of the wing. Use a small circle of black Ultrasuede for the eye, with a dot of white ink for the highlight. Elly's Embellishment Thread in blue can be used for outlining the eye in a stem stitch. Gray Ultrasuede was used for the beak, and a small bit of shading was done with a color pencil in beige on the bottom, near the head.

Detail of Magnolia and Doves block by Sandra L. Mollon
Photo courtesy of The National Quilt Museum

The magnolia flower center is first embroidered with rows of bullion knots in gold double-stranded cotton floss and finished with beads in the center, if desired.

Small white beads were added to the mistletoe, and the wild rose center is finished with bullion knots and French knots in a yellow double-stranded cotton floss. Lastly, add small folded rosebuds and clusters of beads at the end of the narrow branches on the right if desired.

SEASONS OF LIFE

Magnolia and Doves
Upper left quadrant

Center

Block Patterns and Instructions 95

Magnolia and Doves
Upper right quadrant

Center

96   Seasons of Life Quilt

Center

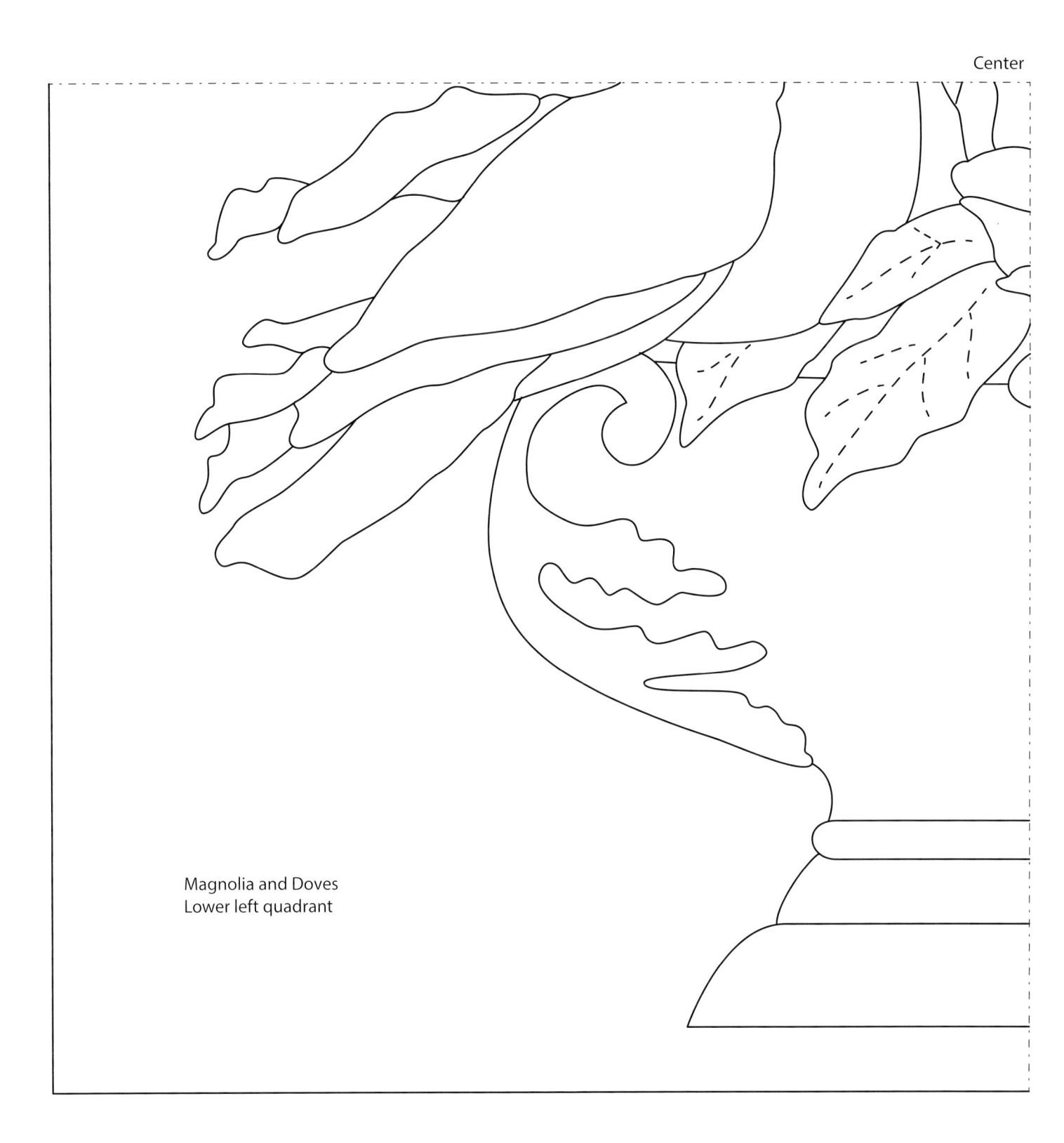

Magnolia and Doves
Lower left quadrant

Center

Magnolia and Doves
Lower right quadrant

98   Seasons of Life Quilt

SEASONS OF LIFE

Block 11: Arts and Crafts Poinsettia Corner

Arts and Crafts Poinsettia Corner block, by Sandra L. Mollon
Photo courtesy of The National Quilt Museum

This corner block is mostly appliqué with some embroidery lines added for leaf veins in some of the leaves. Embroider those in a stem or chain stitch with a single or double thread. The poinsettia flowers were done in various types of red hand-dyed silk.

Detail of Arts and Crafts Poinsettia Corner block by Sandra L. Mollon
Photo courtesy of The National Quilt Museum

Block Patterns and Instructions   99

Arts and Crafts Poinsettia Corner
Block quadrant

Center

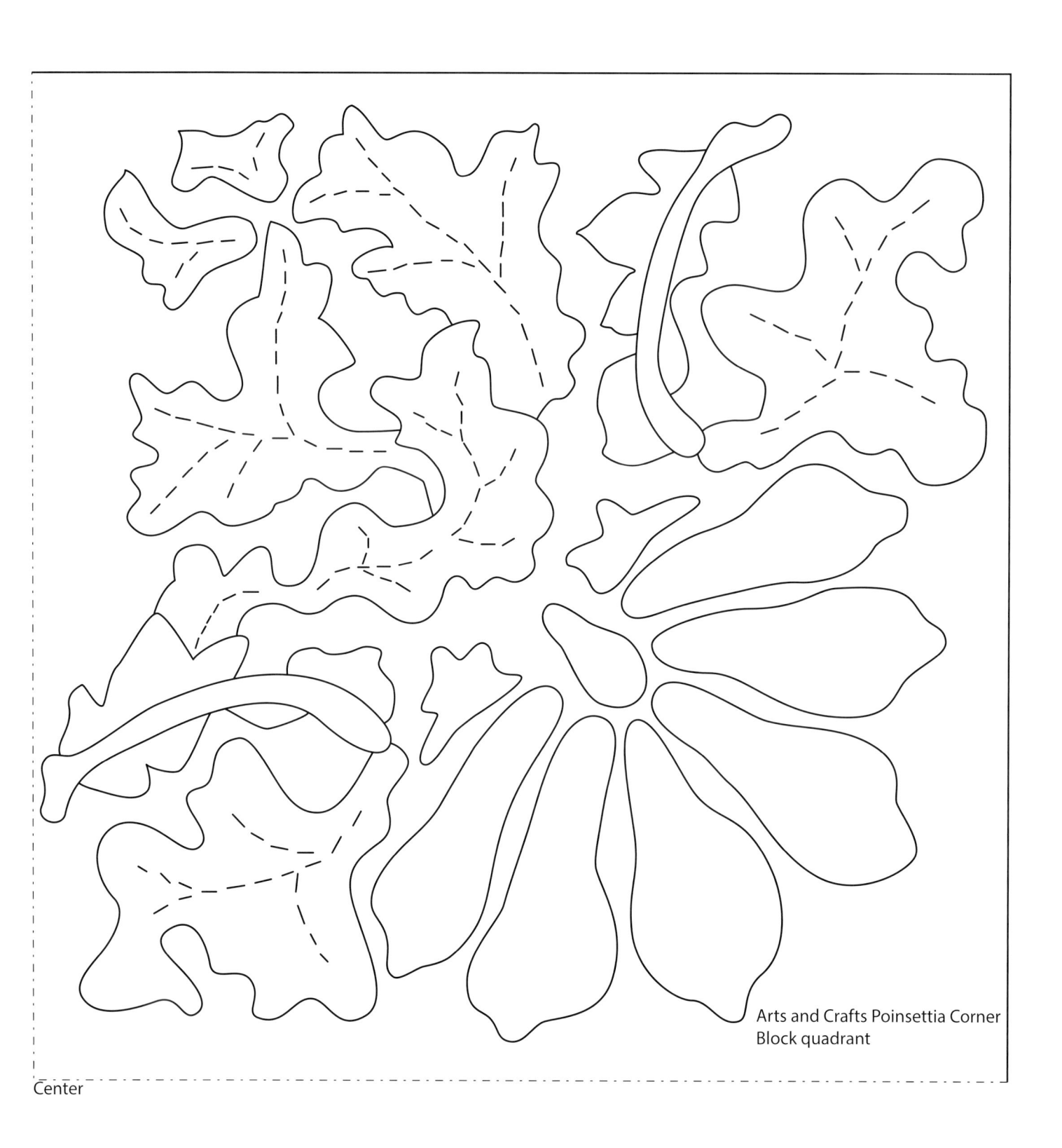

100　Seasons of Life Quilt

Block 12: Circle of Roses

Circle of Roses block, by Sandra L. Mollon
Photo courtesy of The National Quilt Museum

Circle of Roses block by Linda Perricone. Linda used hand-dyed silk velvets for her roses.

As winter turns back to spring, my thoughts went to Valentine's Day, which was the inspiration for this design. I used reds and pinks in my roses and of course added brown stems and green leaves. There are dashed lines on the leaves to indicate where you might embellish with embroidery or simply stitch in quilting lines. For added whimsy, you may want to add an insect, butterfly, or moth. For instructions, see The Bee (page 81).

Circle of Roses
Upper left quadrant

Center

102　Seasons of Life Quilt

SEASONS OF LIFE

Circle of Roses
Upper right quadrant

Center

Block Patterns and Instructions   **103**

Center

Circle of Roses
Lower left quadrant

Seasons of Life Quilt

SEASONS OF LIFE

Center

Circle of Roses
Lower right quadrant

Block Patterns and Instructions **105**

Putting It All Together: Making the Quilt Top

The patterns for the scalloped edge and the center-block appliqué pattern can be found on the pullout (pullout pages P1 and P2).

The Center Block: Ruched Rose in a Crown of Flowers

Ruched Rose in a Crown of Flowers block, by Sandra L. Mollon

Photo courtesy of The National Quilt Museum

1. Begin the center block by preparing the scalloped border. Cut a piece of freezer paper at least 21″ × 21″. Fold in half and then in half again, creasing to make fold lines in the paper. Trace the scalloped-edge pattern on one corner of the freezer paper; then repeat the tracings for the other 3 corners until you have the entire edge drawn. Press the traced sheet to a second sheet with a warm iron to double the freezer paper. Then cut out on the lines and press it to the wrong side of your center-block background fabric. Turn the edges of the fabric as you would any other appliqué shape. Remove the freezer paper.

2. Cut the darker fabric at least 31″ × 31″. Fold it in half and then in half again to find the center. Align the center of the scalloped fabric to the center of the darker square, making sure the scalloped edge is on point. Pin in place, and hand appliqué the scalloped edge to the larger square. Carefully trim away the darker fabric from behind the scalloped center if it leaves a shadow behind the lighter fabric.

SEASONS OF LIFE

3. Once the center square is prepared, appliqué the leaves and flowers in place. Start by making the large ruched rose in the center. Because this flower is large, you may need 2 strips of fabric cut across the width, as a longer strip makes a larger flower. Be sure to hand appliqué the rose to the crinoline before sewing in place on the block. See Ruched Roses (page 26).

4. Make the yo-yos and yo-yo flowers for this block. Add French knots using yellow silk ribbon for the center of the small flowers, or add beads there. The larger leaves were made in 2 pieces from textured fabric. See Pieced Leaves with Textured or Printed Stripes (page 30).

5. Add embroidered veins in the medium-size leaves, if desired, in a chain stitch or stem stitch with single- or double-stranded floss. Or you can add quilting lines later to create the veins.

6. If you wish, add a monogram in the very center of the block. See Resources (page 110) for book recommendations on hand-embroidered monograms.

7. See Pressing the Blocks and Trimming to Size (below) before adding the accent strips.

8. Cut 4 accent strips 1½″ × 30½″. The accent strips are just very narrow borders. Sew them to the block following Sewing Mitered Borders (page 108).

Pressing the Blocks and Trimming to Size

Once the appliqué is complete, press the blocks. To do this, place a clean towel on your ironing board, put the block facedown, and press on the wrong side to smooth the background without crushing the appliqué. Once your block is pressed, trim it down to the finished required size plus the seam allowance. For a finished 15″ × 15″ block, you should trim it down to 15½″ × 15½″, allowing for a ¼″ seam allowance on all sides. I recommend a large square ruler to carefully trim your block. Locate the center of block, double-check it, and mark it with a fine pin. You want to make sure that the design is perfectly centered prior to cutting away extra background fabric. This is very important for the corner blocks because the appliqués need to extend into the corners evenly. The center block is trimmed to 28½″ × 28½″ before adding the accent strips.

TIP If you are using dupioni silk for your background, you can use a serger to both finish and trim the blocks to size. Using a serger is fast and easy, as it secures the edges with an overcast stitch. After the appliqué is complete, cut a 15″ × 15″ square from a sheet of freezer paper, and press it to the wrong side of the finished block, making sure the appliqué design is perfectly centered on the freezer-paper square. Leave the freezer paper on the block; then run the overhanging edges through the serger. Most sergers have a cutting blade that trims the fabric as it sews. Use care to make sure that the overcast edges are just outside of the freezer paper. The edges of the freezer paper are there as a guide to insure you do not trim the block down more than you would like. This may give you a seam allowances that are slightly wider than ¼″, so you may have to adjust your seam allowance width when sewing to accommodate the change. Remove the freezer paper when finished.

SEWING MITERED BORDERS

Sewing mitered borders is something that beginners shy away from, but with practice it becomes easy. We'll start small with the narrow border accent strips around the center block. Find the center of one accent strip and mark with a pin. Measure out 14″ in either direction and place a small dot with a pencil on the accent strip, exactly ¼″ from the raw edge. Do this on both ends.

Using a quilter's ruler with a 45° angle line, place the 45° line along the edge of the accent strip with the dot. The cutting edge of the ruler should be angled out toward the outer edge of the strip and placed exactly ¼″ outside of the sewing line by placing the ruler ¼″ out from the dot marked above.

Check to see that the angle of the ruler is toward the outer corner of the quilt. If you have placed this carefully, you can now trim away the excess fabric, leaving just the ¼″ seam allowance. Measure and trim each end of all 4 border accent strips.

Find the center of each side of the center block and mark with a pin. Measure exactly 14″ in both directions. Mark with a small pencil dot exactly ¼″ away from the edge. Pin an accent strip border to one side, matching the centers and corner dots, and sew from the dot to the dot. Continue to pin and sew all borders. When you have added all 4 borders, you can then pin the mitered corners together and sew from the dot to the outer corner using the same ¼″ seam allowance. Backstitch both at the dot and at the corner to lock in your seams. Press the seam allowances.

The Quilt-Top Center

When all the blocks are complete and trimmed to 15½″ × 15½″, and the center block has the accent strips added to be 30½″ × 30½″, construct the quilt-top center and add the accent strips and borders. Lay out the blocks as suggested in the layout diagram or to your liking.

Using a standard ¼″ seam allowance and matching thread, join the blocks:

- Sew the top row of 4 blocks together, joining the sides.
- Sew the bottom row of 4 blocks together, joining the sides.
- Sew 2 blocks together vertically; repeat with the remaining 2 pairs.
- Sew the pairs to each side of the center block.
- Sew the row above and below the center to the top and bottom of the center section.

The center of your quilt should now measure 60½″ × 60½″ square.

Accent Strip and Borders

The Accent Strip

To add a 1″ finished strip of the darker accent color to all sides of the center, cut 4 strips 1½″ × 62½″. Measure and mark the center of each border and 30″ to each side of the center; mark with a dot. Mark the corner blocks ¼″ inside each outer corner. Follow Sewing Mitered Borders (above) to add the accent strips to the center. The quilt center should now be 62½″ × 62½″.

108 Seasons of Life Quilt

SEASONS OF LIFE

Borders

Detail of corner rose in border by Sandra L. Mollon

Photo courtesy of The National Quilt Museum

Long border strips are often easiest to appliqué before they are sewn to the quilt center because there is less fabric to handle. You probably noticed that the mitered sewing line is partially covered by a large appliquéd rose, so you'll need to appliqué those pieces after the borders are sewn in place.

The border itself finishes at 14˝ wide with mitered corners. The pattern for the border is on the pullout (pullout page P1). Note that it doesn't show the entire width of the dark fabric on the outside edge. Also note that only one corner and one-half of the appliqué border is drawn out. You will need to flip it upside down on a lightbox to trace the remaining half.

1. Prepare a full-size pattern on paper for use in your layout before you begin.

2. Next, make a freezer-paper scalloped-edge template to help make the appliquéd border of the light fabric. Like all of our templates, this is first traced to a single sheet of freezer paper, then pressed to a second piece of freezer paper, and finally cut down on the traced line. It should be the entire length of the side.

3. Prepare your long strips to be appliquéd. If you want to have a dark outer edge with a light scalloped border, as shown, you'll need to cut the dark outside strips of fabric 6½˝ wide by at least 89˝ long. The lighter inside border was cut 9¾˝ wide by 80˝ long for each side, and one edge was scalloped. To make your scalloped edge, press the template onto the wrong side of your light fabric and prepare the edge for appliqué as described for the center block (see The Center Block: Ruched Rose in a Crown of Flowers, Step 2, page 106).

4. Once the edge of your light fabric has scallops, overlap the scalloped edge on top of the dark strip approximately 1˝. Pin in place and appliqué. After this work is finished, carefully trim away the excess dark fabric from under the light scalloped edge, being careful not to cut into the light fabric.

5. Once the scalloped edge is finished, you can begin to add the appliquéd vines and flowers, omitting for now the large flower and leaves in the corner. Make all 4 sides.

6. Mark the center of each side of the quilt. Refer to Sewing Mitered Borders (previous page) to mark the center of each border strip; then measure out 31˝ and mark the dots. Match the border to the quilt at the center and match the corner marks to the previous corner seams. Sew each border to the quilt. Appliqué the large flowers and leaves to the corners.

Notes on Quilting

I (and many of my students) opted for the quilt to be finished by longarm quilting. You may decide to quilt by hand. Study the quilt gallery for quilting ideas. My quilt, with its silk background fabrics and two wool battings, has lots of loft. The roses quilted in the corners of the quilt center were designs taken from the Circle of Roses block. Also note that I added a woven looped cotton trim to the edge, with the edge of the trim enclosed in a bias-cut silk binding.

Detail of quilting around center block done by longarm quilter Kristine Spray on the quilt *Seasons of Life* by Sandra L. Mollon

Photo courtesy of The National Quilt Museum

Congratulations! You have created something beautiful.

Putting It All Together: Making the Quilt Top

Resources

Supplies for Appliqué

Most of the supplies you'll need can be found in your local quilt shop and art supply stores.

ALL-PURPOSE INK, FANTASTIX APPLICATORS, AND FABRICO MARKERS
Tsukineko   tsukineko.co.jp

APPLIQUÉ & PRESSING TOOL
P3 Designs   p3designs.com

BIAS-TAPE MAKERS
Clover USA   clover-usa.com

ELLY'S EMBELLISHMENT THREAD AND YLI SILK THREAD
YLI Threads   ylicorp.com

EMBROIDERY FLOSS
MADEIRA Garne   garne.madeira.de
In addition to cotton floss, I use Madeira Silk floss. It is carried by many United States distributors.

NEEDLES
Good-quality needles are made by several companies. I recommend Bohin, Richard Hemming & Son, and Roxanne needles. Most can be found in local quilt shops or through online retailers.

ROXANNE GLUE-BASTE-IT
Colonial Needle   colonialneedle.com

SILK RIBBON
Cam Creations   silkribbon.com

ULTRASUEDE
Field's Fabrics   fieldsfabrics.com

VALDANI COTTON FLOSS OR PERLE COTTON
Valdani Inc.   valdani.com

Recommended Books

The Art That Is Life, The Arts & Crafts Movement in America, 1875–1920, by Wendy Kaplan (Bulfinch Press)

Silk Quilts: From the Silk Road to the Quilter's Studio, by Hanne Vibeke de Koning-Stapel (Quilt Digest Press)

The Quilter's Appliqué Workshop, by Kevin Kosbab (Interweave)

The Art of Theorem Painting, by Linda Carter Lefko and Barbara Knickerbocker (Crafter's Corner, Inc.)

Monogrammes: L'art des Lettres Brodées, by Susan O'Connor (L'Inédite)
This book is in French but with excellent photographs.

Textiles of the Arts & Crafts Movement, by Linda Parry (Thames & Hudson)

Elly Sienkiewicz's Beloved Baltimore Album Quilts, by Elly Sienkiewicz (C&T Publishing)

Helen M. Stevens' Embroidered Animals, by Helen M. Stevens (David & Charles Publishers)

Treasury of Floral Designs and Initials for Artists and Craftspeople, edited by Mary Carolyn Waldrep (Dover Publications)

About the Author

SANDRA L. MOLLON began making hand appliquéd quilts in 1990. Her work in this genre resulted in the completion of more than ten large hand-appliquéd quilts—many of them hand quilted as well—over two decades.

The work in this book is her first attempt at a design, paired with the challenge of working in mostly all silk, with the resulting quilt becoming a nationally recognized award-winning quilt. It is now a permanent part of The National Quilt Museum collection in Paducah, Kentucky.

Her other interests are fused art quilts, hand dyeing fabric, and thread painting. She holds a bachelor's degree in biology from Central Michigan University and has worked concurrently as both a substitute teacher for middle school and then a high school biology teacher while teaching appliqué on the weekends and sewing for herself and her family.

Visit Sandra online!

WEBSITE: sandramollonquilts.com

Want even more creative content?

Visit us online at ctpub.com

FREE PATTERNS | FREE VIDEO TUTORIALS | TOOLS | GIFTS & MORE!

quilt
snap
share